FORCES AND MOTION

PHYSICS IN ACTION

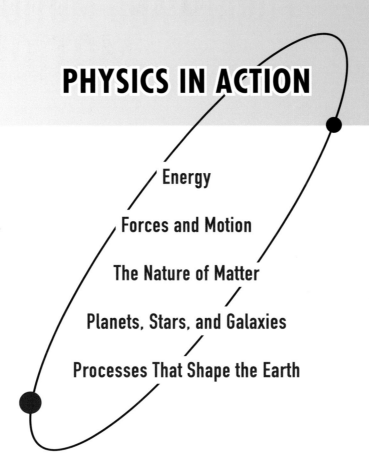

FORCES AND MOTION

Amy Bug

Series Editor
David G. Haase

An imprint of Infobase Publishing

FORCES AND MOTION

Copyright © 2008 by Infobase Publishing

All rights reserved. No part of this book may be reproduced or utilized in any form
or by any means, electronic or mechanical, including photocopying, recording, or by
any information storage or retrieval systems, without permission in writing from the
publisher. For information contact:

Chelsea House
An imprint of Infobase Publishing
132 West 31st Street
New York NY 10001

Library of Congress Cataloging-in-Publication Data
Bug, Amy.
  Forces and motion / Amy Bug.
    p. cm. — (Physics in action)
  Includes bibliographical references and index.
  ISBN-13: 978-0-7910-8931-6 (hardcover)
  ISBN-10: 0-7910-8931-2 (hardcover)
  1. Force and energy. 2. Motion. I. Title. II. Series.

  QC73.B854 2007
  531'.6—dc22

                              2007020737

Chelsea House books are available at special discounts when purchased in bulk quantities for businesses, associations, institutions, or sales promotions. Please call our
Special Sales Department in New York at (212) 967–8800 or (800) 322–8755.

You can find Chelsea House on the World Wide Web at http://www.chelseahouse.com

Text design James Scotto-Lavino
Cover design by Takeshi Takahashi

Printed in the United States of America

Bang NMSG 10 9 8 7 6 5 4 3 2

This book is printed on acid-free paper.

All links and Web addresses were checked and verified to be correct at the time of
publication. Because of the dynamic nature of the Web, some addresses and links may
have changed since publication and may no longer be valid.

Contents

CHAPTER 1

Introduction: The Science of Machines and More

THE TERM *PHYSICS* COMES FROM A GREEK WORD THAT MEANS "knowledge of nature." Physicists are people who study the natural world. The way that physicists have built up their rich knowledge is by combining hands-on experience, philosophical thinking, and mathematics. Sometimes the history of physics was stalled until some crucial type of observation became technologically possible. Sometimes a crucial piece of pure mathematics was developed, and suddenly a whole new world of physics opened up.

This book is about force and motion, which is a subfield of physics called **mechanics**. Mechanics is the oldest branch of physics, in the sense that it was the first one to be put in a form that is fairly complete and recognizable today. The name *mechanics* means that it is about machines. (Today we would say that someone who studies machines is a mechanical engineer.) Before the fifteenth century there was little basic science to guide the design of machines that had been invented much earlier, like the wind and water mills to grind grain, or the cranes used in medieval times to build Europe's cathedrals. These classic machines, which decrease the amount of force a person has to exert, and change one form of motion into another, were well explained by the new science of mechanics.

Also around that time, there was a drive to understand the great "machine" of the planets and stars. "Celestial mechanics" has been studied by people in many parts of the world since the start of recorded history. More than 3,000 years ago, Babylonian scholars compiled detailed records of the positions of the Sun, Moon and stars, though they probably had no theory to knit the observations together. A theory would allow them to deduce new facts and make predictions. For example, if you saw a new planet and charted its position over many nights, could you deduce its distance from Earth and predict its motion for years to come? You could if you had a theory of planetary motion. In approximately A.D. 100, the Egyptian scholar Ptolemy compiled data from earlier observations and combined it with a theory that predicted how the celestial machine would evolve. Unfortunately, it wasn't a correct theory; a glaring error placed the Earth at the center, with the Sun, and everything else in the cosmos, orbiting around it. We generally credit Nicolas Copernicus (around A.D. 1500) with convincingly placing the Sun at the center of our solar system. Interestingly, his ideas were first rejected as heresy, and this is when the word *revolution* (as in "the Earth revolves around the Sun") became a synonym for radical change.[1]

KINEMATICS AND DYNAMICS

The name **kinematics** comes from a Greek word that means "the study of motion". Johannes Kepler, born a few decades after Copernicus died, was apparently the first to correctly understand the kinematics of the planets—that they move, to a very good approximation, in orbits that are shaped like ellipses, with a certain relationship between their speed of motion and the size of the orbit. Sir Isaac Newton, who was born just a few years after Kepler died, later explained why this occurs. Newton gave us **dynamics** (from a Greek word that means "power"). Dynamics explains how force creates the kinematics that we observe.[2] Neptune was discovered in 1846 right where Newton's theory of gravity predicted some previously unknown object must be. In other words, it produced a force that had perturbing effects on the orbit of the planet Uranus, which was already known at that time.[3] More recently, astrophysicists like Vera Rubin have found that a large fraction of the stuff in our universe is "dark matter." It doesn't shine like a star, planet, or gas cloud, with any known type of radiation. Physicists believe dark matter exists because of the detailed way that galaxies rotate around their centers. Some nonvisible type of matter is creating a force that has a very noticeable dynamic effect on the visible matter around it.[4]

Many scholars contributed successfully to mechanics before and during Newton's time. While one can find abundant evidence that his work is based on and interwoven with the work of others, Newton was probably unique among these scholars in the way that he brought observation, philosophy, and mathematics together. It is a powerful synergy that physicists have aspired to ever since. There is something very universal about a physicist's view of the natural world. Newton saw the unity between a rock falling from a tower and the Moon orbiting Earth. They really are two siblings in the same "family" of motions. Both are curves that come from solving a single equation: Force = (mass) × (acceleration). For both, the force is the pull of Earth's gravity. A physics book (this one is no exception) typically considers many situations and applies the same mathematical theory to all of them, showing the unity behind the seeming differences.

ROADMAP FOR THIS BOOK

Chapters 2 through 5 deal with kinematics, while dynamics is discussed in Chapters 6 and 7. Within each chapter you will find the words, math formulas, graphs, and pictures that are all familiar parts of the language of physics. They will take you through the beginning of the kind of mechanics course you might take in the last two years of high school or the first year of college. We do not get to the topics of angular momentum or energy. We also do not talk about Einstein's theories, which are needed for objects moving very swiftly (near the speed of light) and/or subject to very large forces (say, near a massive star).

Every chapter begins with the story of someone dealing with a problematic aspect of motion and/or force. By each chapter's conclusion, we see how the material presented allows them to solve their problem. In Chapter 2, for example, Jaya is challenged to find the average speed of kids hurrying down a long hallway to class. The relationship between speed, time, and distance are made clear with examples, and the concept of displacement is introduced to pave the way for understanding paths that don't necessarily lie along a straight line. In Chapter 3, Oliver and Olivia represent two types of learners, one who is good at manipulating symbols and equations, and one who thinks geometrically. As they use their individual strengths on problems such as when a predator overtakes its prey or how an ecologist measures the speed of water in a stream, they exploit the concept of acceleration, which is the rate of change of speed in time.

In Chapter 4, Tom finds that vectors are an essential ingredient to understanding the velocity of a plane that he must pilot. In that chapter, we represent vectors both with pictures and in terms of their components, and explore how to do algebra with them. We see how displacement, velocity, and acceleration vectors are needed to fully understand interesting motions, and see how a simple accelerometer indicates the strength and direction of acceleration. The importance of acceleration continues in Chapter 5, where Lori and her friends are challenged to find out about the g-forces on a roller coaster. We explore examples like a geosynchronous satellite and a plane that must "touch and go" from a runway.

In Chapter 6, force makes its appearance. Ashok and his friends ponder what would happen if, as in a science-fiction film they've seen, someone is expelled into outer space. The nature of motion in the absence of any force (as when one is floating in space) is discussed and explained in terms of Newton's first law.

The important concept of center-of-mass is introduced as well. Pressure forces are explained, and Ashok understands the importance of both gravity and atmospheric pressure to keep the human body in healthful balance.

Finally, in Chapter 7, Newton's second and third laws are presented. In that chapter, Molly thinks about the meaning of inertia, or mass, and the rule that an object feeling a force will experience an acceleration inversely proportional to its inertia. While concerned with keeping the child that she is babysitting out of harm's way, Molly does a skillful calculation using all three of Newton's laws and the vector nature of velocity, in order to understand the consequences of a collision between a pedestrian and a vehicle.

CHAPTER 2

Getting from Here to There: Describing Motion with Words, Pictures, and Equations

JAYA'S HIGH SCHOOL HAS A REALLY LONG HALLWAY THAT everyone calls the "infinite corridor."[5] Obviously, the hall is not infinitely long, but it feels that way to students who are late to class. It sure felt that way to Jaya and her friends, who were playing their usual post-lunchtime game of basketball when the 2-minute warning bell rang for fourth period. Jaya grabbed her backpack and dashed down the hallway. Her friend Jamal made it in 2 minutes flat. Jaya was next as she slid, as casually as possible, into her seat. She had made it in 2½ minutes. It took their third friend, John, a full 3½ minutes.

Their teacher, Dr. Kelp, came and stood before them, examining them as if they were the physics experiment of the day. (It turns out that they were.) Dr. Kelp made a deal with them that if they would go to the board and work out their average speeds during their trip from the basketball court, there would be no penalty for being late. "You need to know the length of the corridor, which is 1/6th of a mile." said Dr. Kelp. "Since physicists use the SI system of units, please work out your average speed in kilometers per second."

Determining the **average speed** of a body in motion is just one of the applications of physics. This chapter will discuss the concept of average speed, and how it is used in everyday life.

DEFINING THE AVERAGE SPEED

Suppose that you notice a dog trotting by the side of a country highway. It is the kind of a highway where there are some markers every 1/10 of a mile. Suppose you catch sight of the dog starting to run at a marker that says "20 miles" and you watch it run past 3 more markers (as in Figure 2.1). The distance that the dog has run is

$$\text{Distance traveled} = (3)(1/10 \text{ mile}) = 0.3 \text{ mile}$$

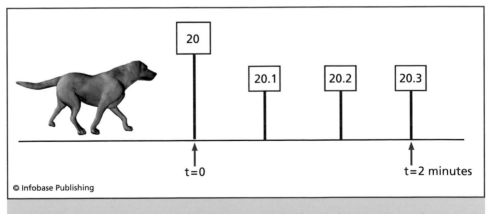

© Infobase Publishing

Figure 2.1 *A dog running past distance markers by the road. It travels past four markers in a time period of* t = 2 min. *The markers are 1/10 mile apart.*

Let's say that the time it takes for the dog to do this is 2 minutes:

Time spent = 2 minutes

The average speed of anything moving is the distance traveled divided by the time spent, as in the following equation:

Average speed = distance traveled/time spent

Before we plug in numbers, let's talk about how to rewrite this equation in a way that uses the conventional language of physics.

TALKING ABOUT PHYSICS: DIMENSIONS AND UNITS

When we talk about the **dimensions** of a quantity, we mean "What type of real-world quantity is it?" There are three fundamental dimensions in mechanics: length, mass, and time. For example, when we say that "The distance the dog has run is 0.3 mile," the dimension of the number 0.3 is length. When someone says, "Where have you been? I've been waiting 20 minutes," 20 has the dimension of time. Sometimes, a quantity doesn't have any dimensions; it is a pure number. For example, the five in the statement "Watch, I can fit five cookies in my mouth all at once!" is a pure number. The number "π" in the statement, "A circle's circumference is π times the diameter," is also a pure number.

If we said that "The diameter of the circle is 10 meters, so its area is 25π meters^2," the diameter, 10, has dimensions of length, and its area, 25π, has dimensions of (length)^2. We can take fundamental dimensions of length, mass, and time and combine them, using the rules of algebra to get new dimensions.

The quantity of average speed, defined above, has dimensions of (length/time).

A concept related to dimensions is **units**. A meter is a unit of the dimension length, as is a mile. In physics, when we write a real-world quantity that has dimensions, we need to associate units with it. If my friend said that her brother was 18, I might think he was 18 years old. But if I went over to her house and saw that the brother was a baby, I'd realize that she meant 18 months instead. Often we write units using abbreviations, such as "yrs" for years and "m" for meter.

We can do arithmetic to transform one unit to another. A conversion factor is a number that gives us the proportionality of two different units. For example,

$$1 \text{ mile} = 1609 \text{ meters} \qquad \text{so}$$
$$0.3 \text{ mile} = (0.3 \text{ mile}) (1609 \text{ m})/(1 \text{ mile})$$
$$= (0.3 \cancel{\text{ mile}}) (1609 \text{ m})/(1 \cancel{\text{ mile}}) = (0.3)(1609) \text{ m}$$
$$= 482.7 \text{ m} \quad \textit{Distance run by dog in meters}$$

Notice how the math operation, division, gets done on the units as well as on the numbers. In this way, the conversion factor (1609 m/ 1 mile) does its job of converting the mile unit into the meter unit, because it makes the miles cancel out.

There are many systems of units available for use. One system that is widely used in physics is the **Système Internationale (SI)**, which measures length in meters (m), time in seconds (s), and mass in kilograms (kg). We will use these units in addition to other units, such as time in hours, days, or years. In fact, if we are talking about astrophysics, the length of a day (which is the time for a planet to rotate on its axis) or a year (the time to revolve once around the Sun) depend on what planet you are on.

A Day and a Year in the Life of Planets

How long is a day? How long is a year? It depends on what planet you call home. Table 2.1 lists the time it takes for a planet to rotate on its axis (day), and the time it takes for a planet to orbit once around its sun (year). As you see, there is no pattern to how long a day is. (On Venus, days are longer than years!) On the other hand, how long a year lasts follows directly from how far the planet is from the Sun. The relationship is called Kepler's third law. Kepler's third law explains that planets farther from the Sun travel slower in their orbits than planets closer to the Sun.

TABLE 2.1	Planets and the Length of Their Days, Their Years, and Distance from the Sun		
PLANET	**DAY (IN EARTH DAYS)**	**YEAR (IN EARTH YEARS)**	**DISTANCE FROM SUN (IN EARTH DISTANCES)**
Mercury	58.7	0.24 (88 earth days)	0.39
Venus	243.0	0.61 (223 earth days)	0.72
Mars	1.03	1.88	1.52
Jupiter	9.8	11.86	5.20
Saturn	10.2	29.46	9.54
Uranus	17.9	84.01	19.18
Neptune	19.1	164.8	30.06
Pluto*	6.4	248.6	39.53
*Smaller than a true planet, Pluto is currently considered a dwarf planet.			

TALKING ABOUT PHYSICS: USING SYMBOLS

The equation

Average speed = distance traveled/time spent

is something that we'd like to express by writing algebraic symbols instead of words. There is a tradition in the way we choose our symbols in physics. The word **velocity** (from the Greek word *velox*, meaning "fast") is a favorite one in physics, and we typically pick a symbol with a "*v*" for some type of speed. We often use subscripts to tell ourselves more about a quantity or to distinguish two quantities which are related in some way. So we write v_{ave} for average speed (later we will talk about a second kind of speed, the instantaneous speed). We use the symbol t for time. Moreover, since "time spent" is a time interval, which is a difference in two times, we use a pairing of two symbols, Δt, to stand for this difference. (This might be a tradition that you see in your math classes as well.) The Δ is a Greek letter called *delta* and represents a difference in something. So Δt is a time difference, and Δd is a distance difference. The equation using symbols looks like

$$v_{ave} = \Delta d / \Delta t \qquad (2.1)$$

As we said above, we often use subscripts in physics to denote related quantities. For example, the dog is seen at two different distances, 20 miles and then 20.3 miles along the highway. The first location can be symbolized as d_i, and the second location can be symbolized as d_f. The subscript i stands for initial, and the subscript f stands for final, another physics convention. Putting our different symbols together, we have

$$\Delta d = d_f - d_i = (20.3 - 20) \text{ miles} = 0.3 \text{ miles}$$

and

$$\Delta t = t_f - t_i = 2 \text{ minutes}$$

FINDING THE AVERAGE SPEED

For the dog trotting along,

$$\Delta d = 0.3 \text{ mile and } \Delta t = 2 \text{ minutes}$$

When we insert these numbers into our equation for average speed, Equation 2.1, we get a result

$$v_{ave} = 0.3 \text{ mile/2 minutes} = 0.15 \text{ mile/minute}$$

This is a pretty good speed for a domestic animal!

We have used units in creating our equation. Now, what units should you use to write a result? The answer: Any units you wish, as long as they have the right dimensions. For a speed like the speed of the dog, the units should have the dimension of a length over a time. Sometimes the person doing the calculation will prefer to get the result in one kind of unit. Suppose you are driving alongside the dog and matching your speed to it. If your car has a speedometer that gives km/hour, you would see the dog's speed in those units. (One kilometer, abbreviated km, is equal to 1000 m.) We can use conversion factors to convert the speed to any other units, say, km/hour:

$$v_{ave} = (1.6 \text{ km/mile})(0.15 \text{ miles/minute})(60 \text{ minutes/1 hour})$$
$$= 14.4 \text{ km/hour}$$

SPEED, TIME, OR DISTANCE?

We can turn the speed problem inside out, and ask that if we move at a certain average speed, how long does it take to travel a certain distance? The answer is:

$$\text{Time spent} = \text{distance traveled/average speed}$$

Or, in symbols, from Equation 2.1:

$$\Delta t = \Delta d / v_{ave} \tag{2.2}$$

For example, light travels at an enormous speed. (Light moves through the vacuum of space at constant speed with no slowing down or speeding up.) It is conventional to use the symbol c when we refer to the speed of light, which is

$$c = 299{,}792{,}458 \text{ meters/sec}$$

Suppose that on a cloudless night, we shine a powerful laser at the Moon. How long does it take this light to reach the Moon, which is around 385,000,000 meters away? (This will be an estimate, since Δd, the Earth-Moon distance, varies a little bit throughout the month and the year.) Equation 2.2 would tell us that

$$\Delta t = \Delta d / v_{ave}$$
$$= \Delta d / c = 385{,}000{,}000 \text{ meters}/(299{,}792{,}458 \text{ meters/sec})$$
$$= 1.28 \text{ seconds}$$

Similarly, if we know the time spent and the average speed, we can solve for distance traveled:

$$\Delta d = v_{ave} \, \Delta t \tag{2.3}$$

For example, a young man usually walks to school, but one day he gets a ride in his friend's car. He walks at an average speed of v_{walk} = 5 miles/hour, and his friend drives at v_{drive} = 25 miles/hour. If it takes the young man a time Δt = 3 minutes to get to school in the car, how far is the school? How long would it have taken him to walk? In answer to the first question, the distance to school is

$$\Delta d = (3 \text{ minutes})(25 \text{ miles/hour})(1 \text{ hour}/60 \text{ minutes})$$
$$= 1.25 \text{ miles}$$

In answer to the second question, we could plug $\Delta d = 1.25$ miles into Equation 2.2. More interestingly, we could observe that the time it takes is inversely proportional to the speed. In other words, the time to walk would be $(3 \text{ minutes})(v_{drive} / v_{walk}) = 15$ minutes.

The important thing to keep in mind is that given any two of the quantities distance, time, and average speed, we can find the third one. Interestingly, when scientists in the seventeenth century were trying to decide how to describe motion, they came up with even a fourth quantity. They were not sure whether it was better to write Equation 2.1, which shows distance per amount of time spent, $v_{ave} = \Delta d/\Delta t$, or to show the time per amount of distance traveled:

$$X = \Delta t/\Delta d \qquad\qquad (2.4)$$

They eventually decided on describing motion with Equation 2.1. Of course, X is related to v_{ave} because $X = 1/v_{ave}$. Do you agree with their decision? That is, of Equations 2.1 and 2.4, which do you think is a superior way to describe motion?

DISTANCE OR DISPLACEMENT? A DECISION ABOUT WHAT SPEED REALLY MEANS

Motion does not have to be in a straight line for Equations 2.1 to 2.3 to work. But if not, a complication arises. We have to decide what we mean by the distance we travel, and what we want "average speed" to tell us. For example, suppose that our path is the zig-zagging motion that a taxi would take driving through the streets (running east to west) and avenues (running north to south) of New York City. Suppose that each street block is 1/5 mile long, while each avenue block is 1/20 mile long. The taxi goes 20 blocks north and 3 blocks east. Traffic is terrible; the ride takes 25 minutes. What is the average speed, v_{ave}, of the taxi? If we use the idea that $\Delta d = d_f - d_i$ is the final location minus the initial location, we want the "straight-line" distance traveled between the two points. This is the hypotenuse of the triangle drawn on Figure 2.2. We would want

$$\Delta d = \sqrt{a^2 + b^2}$$

where $a = 20(1/20)$ mile and $b = 3 (1/5)$ mile. So

$$\Delta d = 1.17 \text{ miles}$$

Therefore,

$$v_{ave} = \Delta d/\Delta t = 1.17 \text{ miles}/25 \text{ mins}$$
$$= 0.047 \text{ miles/minute}$$
$$= 2.8 \text{ miles/hour}$$

Depending on how athletic you are, it might be better to just run! But what if you knew that you could run at, say, 3.0 miles/hour, for as much as 25 minutes straight. Would you beat the taxi? No, because you (and the taxi) would not be moving along a straight path of $d_f - d_i = 1.17$ miles. Instead, you would be zig-zagging along a that had a larger total distance, because it followed the pattern of the New York streets and avenues. The distance that the taxi actually covered along the

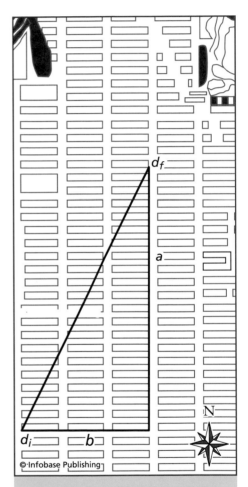

Figure 2.2 *The grid of streets (horizontal) and avenues (vertical) in part of New York City.*

streets and avenues is $D = a + b$, where $a = 20\ (1/20)$ mile and $b = 3\ (1/5)$ mile. So

$$D = 20\ (1/20)\ \text{mile} + 3\ (1/5)\ \text{mile} = 1.6\ \text{miles}$$

This suggests a second definition of the rate at which something moves. Let's call it s. If you were concerned about whether you could beat the taxi, s would tell you the speed to beat:

$$s = D/\Delta t = 1.6\ \text{miles}/25\ \text{minutes} = 0.064\ \text{miles/minute}$$
$$= 3.8\ \text{miles/hour}$$

The taxi follows a zig-zag path of length s, made of straight line segments. We can also talk about curved paths. For example, Earth orbits around the Sun in a motion that takes about 365 days. Its path is (roughly) circular with a radius of 150,000,000 km (Figure 2.3). What is Earth's average speed in orbit?

Here again, we have the choice: Do we want the kind of average speed that tells us about covering the straight-line distance between two endpoints, or do we want the rate to cover the actual distance traveled, D? In the first case, $\Delta d = d_f - d_i = 0$ for a complete orbit. Using Equation 2.1, we would say

$$v_{ave} = 0\ \text{over the time of one orbit}$$

Since $D = 2\pi r$ is the distance around the circumference of a circle with radius r, the second kind of speed is

$$s = D/\Delta t = (2\pi)150{,}000{,}000\ \text{km}/365\ \text{days}$$

Multiplying s by the conversion factor (1 day/24 hours) and also by the conversion factor (1 hour/3600 seconds) is one way to find the speed in km/sec. Namely:

$$s = 29.9\ \text{km/sec}$$

So the average speed in one orbit is zero. But 29.9 km/sec, or about 66,900 miles/hour (!) tells how fast we go as we ride with Earth around the Sun during a year.

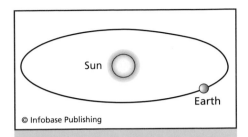

Figure 2.3 *Earth follows a roughly circular orbit around the Sun with radius r = 150,000,000 km.*

For this orbit problem, the rate s seems to be much more useful than v_{ave}. However, it is displacement, Δd, over the time, v_{ave} of Equation 2.1, that is always introduced in physics texts. Why do they neglect s? The answer is that they don't. It just shows up under another name. We will return to this in Chapter 3, where we'll see that it is related to an even more general quantity called v, the instantaneous speed.

We need some terminology to keep the two different kinds of distance and speed straight. In physics, we use the term **displacement** for Δd, the distance along a hypothetical straight line from the starting point to the ending point of a motion. If we need to refer to a quantity like D, which is the length of the actual path traversed by someone or something, we will from now on call it the **path length**.

The way displacement and path length relate to each other can be seen on the trail map in Figure 2.4a. Suppose that a hiker decides to hike from the trail head to the waterfall, starting on the Upper Camp Lane trail and then, below cabin 1, taking the Lower Camp Lane trail. The path length from the trail head to the waterfall along that route is $D = 3.6$ km. It takes him a time of $\Delta t = 1$ hour to cover the distance. So the answer to the question of how fast the hiker is able to cover this terrain is $s = D/\Delta t = 3.6$ km/hr. But the displacement between the trail head and waterfall is $\Delta d = 3.0$ km (Figure 2.4b). So the hiker's average speed is $v_{ave} = 3.0$ km/hr.

There are a few alternative paths on the map that the hiker could take. For example, the Upper Pine Forest trail looks shorter

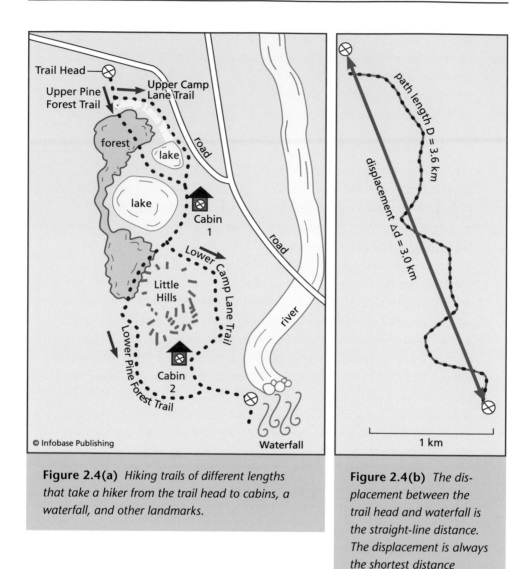

Figure 2.4(a) *Hiking trails of different lengths that take a hiker from the trail head to cabins, a waterfall, and other landmarks.*

Figure 2.4(b) *The displacement between the trail head and waterfall is the straight-line distance. The displacement is always the shortest distance between two points.*

than the Upper Camp Lane trail. Each hiking path has a different path length D, but for all paths between the trail head and waterfall $\Delta d = 3.0$ km. Suppose one hiker had a choice of many trails. It is v_{ave} that tells which is a faster trail. Since Δd is the same for all choices of trails, the trail that takes this hiker the smallest amount of time, Δt in Equation 2.1, is fastest and it will be the one with the largest v_{ave}.

On the other hand, s has a purpose, too. It reveals when a person is a faster hiker. If many people hiked these trails, and we timed each person, regardless of his or her route, the person who hiked the trail in the shortest time, Δt, is probably the one who we'd call fastest. They would have the largest speed, s.

Finding the best path between known endpoints, perhaps visiting known intermediate points, too, is an important real-world problem. There can be different definitions of "best path." For a hiker anxious to get to the end of the trail, the best path might be the one with the largest v_{ave} (which is, all other things being equal, the shortest path). Similarly, communications companies want to know how to wire networks using the least length of wire. Electronics manufacturers want to know how to drill holes in circuit boards so that their robotic drills take the shortest path, and therefore have the highest average speed over the circuit board. One of the classic problems of this type is the "traveling salesman problem," in which a person spends time visiting a certain number of cities, visiting each city just once, and finishes up at the initial city. The problem considers in what order the person should visit the cities to minimize the distance traveled.[6] Say you wanted to design a new trail for hikers. You want it to visit the trail head, visit cabin 1, cabin 2, the waterfall, and return to the trail head. A little thought suggests that the shortest path will be made entirely of straight-line segments that connect these points. But there is choice in the order in which you visit these landmarks resulting in different set of line segments. If you found the shortest path of line segments that did this, you would have solved a classic traveling salesman problem.

CARTOON MOTION

Almost everyone has seen a flip book, a book with a series of pictures that you hold with one hand and flip through its pages with the thumb of the other. The images change very gradually from one page to the next page, so that when you flip through it, the book gives the illusion of motion. Maybe this is what the ancient Greek philosopher Parmenides had in mind when he proposed that nothing really moves—that motion is an illusion.[7] In the ancient world, people struggled with the question "How do things move through space and time?" Like Parmenides, some people were not even sure that motion was real. The philosopher Zeno argued that motion can't happen because to cover a distance, you have to cover half of it, then half of the remaining half, then half of half of the remaining half, and so on. So you will never be able to actually achieve a distance! (What do you say to his argument?)

If you flip slowly through a flip book, the images appear to jump. But if you flip fast enough, your eyes and brain will tell you that the motion is continuous. The motion is an optical illusion. The basics of why it occurs are not fully understood even today. Psychologists have given it the name "short-range apparent motion." It is related to, but not the same as, flicker fusion, which refers to the fact that if a light goes on and off quickly enough, your eyes don't see the change in brightness.[8] Most people experience flicker fusion at around 70 flashes a second.

You can consider each image in a flip book a frame, like the frames that animators use in creating cartoons. The term *frame rate* means how many unique frames, or still images, you are flashing in front of a viewer's eyes per unit time. The units that animators use are frames per second (fps). You can get away with showing a human viewer much less than 70 fps and have them see the motion as realistic. Live-action movies are filmed and shown in theatres at a rate of 24 fps, with motion still looking natural. With computer-generated animation, studios like Pixar (*The Incredibles*) or Dreamworks Animation SKG (*Shrek*) combine artistic and mathematical skill in computer programs that, though the final product is still limited to 24 fps, also make motion look natural.

CONCLUSION: RUNNING IN THE HALL

Their physics teacher, Dr. Kelp, smiled as the students worked together to calculate their average speeds and then wrote these correct answers on the blackboard (Table 2.2).

TABLE 2.2 Jaya's Answers			
NAME	Δt (min)	v_{ave} (mile/min)	v_{ave} (km/sec)
Jamal	2.0	1/12	0.0022
Jaya	2.5	1/15	0.0018
John	3.5	1/21	0.0013

Formulas: $v_{ave} = \Delta d/\Delta t$
$\Delta d = 1/6$ mile
1.6 km = 1 mile
60 sec = 1 minute

The concept of average speed is an important one in everyday life. It pulls together ideas of distance and time in a very helpful way. The examples in this chapter use average speed to describe everything from the rate that a person travels to school, to the rate that a planet travels in its orbit, to the time that it takes light to travel across space. This is an example of the unity of physics. We can think up countless situations, and the same rule applies to all of them. This is the reason why physics is so meaningful and so exciting to contemplate.

CHAPTER 3

Speeding Up and Slowing Down: The Relationship Between Speed and Acceleration

Oliver and Olivia are twins, born 8 minutes apart. Their birthday seems to be about the only thing they have in common. Oliver plays football; Olivia does ballet. Olivia is a vegetarian; Oliver holds the school record for most hamburgers consumed during one lunch period (almost six). In physics class, they always take different approaches to solving problems.

Dr. Kelp's physics class was given a problem to solve on the motion of a predator and its prey. At time $t = 0$, a hungry jaguar takes off after a mouse. The class needed to find the time it took for the jaguar to reach the mouse. For extra credit, they could find the speeds of each animal at that moment. Olivia took her favorite approach of writing equations. She copied down the equation that Dr. Kelp had placed on the board, which described the jaguar's position measured in meters, at time (t) measured in seconds:

$$x_{jaguar} = t^2 - 10$$

She copied the second equation that described the mouse's position:

$$x_{mouse} = 3t$$

She then wrote a third equation that set them equal to each other:

$$x_{jaguar} = x_{mouse}$$

In other words,

$$t^2 - 10 = 3t$$

Olivia was able to simplify this equation and find out the time, t, when the positions of the mouse and jaguar coincided.

After he copied the equations from the board, Oliver took his favorite approach of drawing graphs. He drew some axes and labeled the vertical one x and the horizontal one t. He drew two curves using these axes and called them $x_{jaguar}(t)$ and $x_{mouse}(t)$. Then he saw where the curves crossed. The time, t, where they crossed is when the jaguar and mouse coincided (Figure 3.1).

Both Oliver and Olivia got the same, correct answer. (They usually both get the right

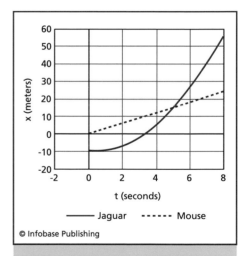

© Infobase Publishing

Figure 3.1 *Oliver's graph of position, x, versus time, t, for the mouse and the jaguar. The mouse's position, x$_{mouse}$(t) is shown by the dashed line; the jaguar's, x$_{jaguar}$(t), by the red line.*

answer; it's one additional thing that they have in common.) But they arrived at the answer in what might seem to be totally different ways. Graphs and equations are two useful and complementary ways of understanding motion. In this chapter we will use them to talk about **instantaneous speed**. (This is an extension of the concept of average speed from Chapter 2.) We will also explore motion during which the instantaneous speed is changing, or **accelerated motion**.

CONSTANT AVERAGE SPEED: POSITION VERSUS TIME IS A STRAIGHT LINE

The graph in Figure 3.1 tells us the positions of the mouse (dashed line) and jaguar (red line) at any moment. If Dr. Kelp had given the class that graph to begin with, and asked them where the animals were at some time, they could just read off their positions. For example, at time $t = 0$, the mouse is at position 0 and the jaguar at −10 meters. At time $t = 2$ seconds, the mouse is found at 6 meters, and the jaguar is at −6 meters, and so on. The graph of the mouse's position is particularly distinctive—it's just a straight line. When an object moves at a constant average speed, its graph of distance versus time is always a straight line. Where the graph crosses the vertical axis (called the "y intercept") tells you where the object was at time $t = 0$. The line's slope is positive if the object moves in the positive direction, and negative if moves in the negative direction. The size of the slope tells you

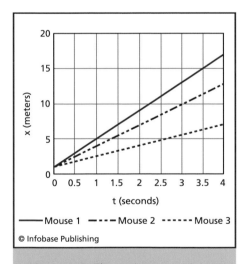

Figure 3.2 *The positions, x, of three mice versus time, t.*

TABLE 3.1   Time and Position of Mice in Figure 3.2

TIME (sec)	POSITION (m) MOUSE 1	POSITION (m) MOUSE 2	POSITION (m) MOUSE 3
0.0	1.0	1.0	1.0
1.0	5.0	4.0	2.5
2.0	9.0	7.0	4.0
3.0	13.0	10.0	5.5
4.0	17.0	13.0	7.0

about the average speed. For example, Figure 3.2 graphs the motion of three different mice that all start from $x = 1$ meter at time $t = 0$. Table 3.1 shows the time and corresponding position of each mouse that is shown on the graph.

The mouse that goes a longer distance, Δd, in a given amount of time, Δt, has a higher average speed, since $v_{ave} = \Delta d/\Delta t$. Therefore, we would order their speeds in this way: Mouse 1 is faster than Mouse 2, which is faster than Mouse 3. From Table 3.1, we can find the values of each mouse's average speed. It doesn't matter which pair of times for each mouse we pick out of the table and use for $\Delta t = t_f - t_i$. Because the average speed is constant, any choice gives the same answer. So for the mice:

$$v_{ave} = \Delta d/\Delta t = 4 \text{ m/sec (Mouse 1)}, 3 \text{ m/sec (Mouse 2)},$$
$$1.5 \text{ m/sec (Mouse 3)}$$

To summarize: when the position versus time graph is a straight line, its slope is just v_{ave}.

INSTANTANEOUS SPEED

In Chapter 2, we noted that the average speed, v_{ave}, doesn't always tell you how fast an object is moving at any given time. The quantity s seemed better at this for the taxi or the orbiting planet.

In physics, an object executes **uniform motion** if it moves in a straight line at a constant average speed, like the three mice in Figure 3.2. Olivia likes to think of a uniform motion as one where the ratio of $\Delta d/\Delta t$ is the same at all times during the motion. Oliver prefers to think of the graph of distance versus time as being a straight line. But this isn't true for the taxi or the orbiting planet in Chapter 2. We'd like to be able to talk about a non-uniform motion where the distance (Δd) covered in a certain time interval (Δt) changes as the motion proceeds or where motion deviates from a straight line, or both!

Logically, there is nothing wrong with saying that during a non-uniform motion, v_{ave} depends explicitly on both t_f and t_i, the starting and ending times of each time interval Δt. But there is a better way to characterize the speed. Taking the time interval Δt to be very short (an "instant" if you will) is a most useful and interesting tactic. Then the two numbers t_f and t_i are virtually the same. This will lead us to the idea of the instantaneous speed, or just speed for short, symbolized in this book as v.

It is good to keep in mind, though, that if the rate at which distance is covered is constant in time, the instantaneous and average speeds will agree. For example, a car that cruises in a straight line down a highway with a speedometer that reads a steady 55 mph has $s = v_{ave} = v = 55$ miles/hr. Its position on a graph would look like one of the lines in Figure 3.2, in that it would be a straight line whose slope indicated 55 mi/hr. But cars readily change speed, and the purpose of a car's speedometer is to measure its instantaneous speed (v). When driving in many places, it is fairly important that not just the average speed stay below 55 miles/hour, but that the instantaneous speed does too. If you are stopped for speeding, it will not help to tell the police officer "I may have been speeding for the last 5 minutes, but for the 5 minutes before that, I was going under the speed limit. So please use physics, officer, and you will find my average speed (v_{ave}) over $\Delta t = 10$ minutes was okay!"

To find instantaneous speed, we take a very short time interval and ask how far something moves in that time. The crucial difference between this idea and the idea of finding average speed is that the time interval is really short, as short as you can possibly imagine. Then

Instantaneous speed = short distance traveled/short time

In symbols,

$$v = \delta d/\delta t \qquad\qquad (3.1)$$

In Equation 3.1, δ is the lowercase form of the Greek letter delta. We use it to symbolize a very small quantity. This tradition stems from Gottfried Leibnitz, who was the co-creator of the branch of math known as *calculus*. It is guaranteed by Leibnitz's calculus that the limit of vanishingly short times and paths is a sensible concept and that the ratio in Equation 3.1 can come out to be a finite number.

A nice consequence of using Equation 3.1 is that the (potentially confusing) distinction between D and Δd, and between s and v_{ave}, is unnecessary. Consider a very short time period $t_f - t_i = \Delta t$. During that time, an object has the opportunity to move only a very short distance, with $d_f - d_i = \Delta d$. As you can convince yourself by drawing a curved line on paper, and then isolating smaller and smaller segments of it, a very short segment of a curve looks very much like a straight line. Thus Δd represents the length of that segment in the limit that it is a short, perfectly straight line. Thus, the path distance and displacement, D and Δd, will be identical:

$D = \Delta d = \delta d$ in the limit that δt becomes extremely small

In this limit,

$$s = v_{ave} = v \qquad \text{for } s \text{ and } v_{ave} \text{ calculated during the time interval } \delta t$$

OLIVER AND OLIVIA FIND THE INSTANTANEOUS SPEED

The speed of flowing water is very important in determining what kinds of animals and plants can survive in the ecosystem of a river or stream. If water flows too slowly, the availability of oxygen is a problem. If the water flows too quickly (and especially if it develops turbulence), it creates a problem for structurally delicate plants and animals. Oliver and Olivia became interested in an article they read in their environmental science class about the ecology of a stream that happens to be near their house. One ecologist dropped a stick at the point where the tiny, winding stream bubbles up out of the ground. The stick floated along with the water, and a second ecologist with a stopwatch walked alongside it. He had a stopwatch and a pedometer (a device to measure the distance a person walks or runs). Every once in a while, he could record the time and the distance (D) the stick had traveled. The first ecologist had taken the numbers and graphed the distance traveled by the stick (Figure 3.3).

Olivia and Oliver set themselves the task of finding the instantaneous speed (v) of the water over this time. For example, how fast was the stick moving during, roughly, the first two minutes? This was easy, because that portion of the graph of distance (D) versus time (t) is a straight line. Its slope is roughly $v_{ave} = v = 70$ m/2 min = 0.6 m/sec. How about from 2 to 4 minutes? The stick seems to have caught on an obstacle (perhaps the bank or tree roots) and its instantaneous speed is $v = 0$ during that time period.

The twins next wanted to tackle the last minute on the graph. During that minute, the stick was definitely not moving with a constant speed. The article did not show enough detail for them to judge the instantaneous speed though; the dots were too few and too far apart in time. They emailed one of the ecologists, who emailed back an extremely detailed graph (Figure 3.4a) of the stick's distance during the time period from 4 to 5 minutes. His new graph contained so much new data that a fairly smooth curve was drawn (which went through the dots from the original article).

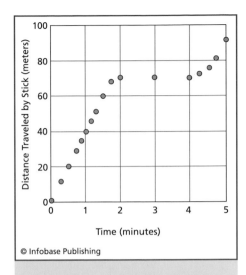

Figure 3.3 *The distance traveled by a stick that floats down a small stream. The stick is an indicator of the speed of the water.*

The twins realized they could use the formula of Equation 3.1, $v = \delta d / \delta t$. Olivia said, "Let's find the speed at $t = 4$ minutes and 30 seconds." Oliver replied, "Okay, and let's use $\delta t = 20$ seconds." He took his pencil and with a straight edge drew a line segment that spanned the 20 seconds around the time $t = 4$ minutes, 30 seconds. Oliver's line segment crosses the curve at $t = 4$ minutes, 20 seconds and again at $t = 4$ minutes, 40 seconds (Figure 3.4b).

Oliver then read the two appropriate position values off the graph and did the math:

$$\delta d = x \text{ (4 minutes, 40 seconds)} - x \text{ (4 minutes, 20 seconds)}$$
$$= (79 - 72.5) \text{ meters} = 6.5 \text{ meters}$$

Therefore, $v = 6.5$ meters/20 seconds = 0.33 meters/sec.

"Hey, I've found that $v = 0.33$ meters/sec is the slope of the line," said Oliver. "This is the speed of the water at time of $t = 4\frac{1}{2}$

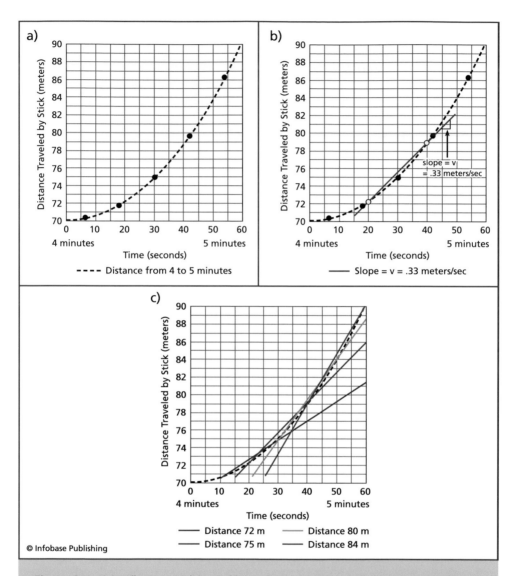

Figure 3.4 *(a) A floating stick is used by ecologists to determine the water speed by recording the distance of the stick from its origin during the time from 4 to 5 minutes. The small circles represent the data in Figure 3.3, but more data has been recorded here to create the dashed line. Points can now be connected to form what looks like a smooth curve. (b) Oliver drew a straight line that crosses the distance curve at t = 4 minutes, 20 seconds and t = 4 minutes, 40 seconds. The slope of the line gives a good estimate of the speed of the stick at a time of 4 minutes and 30 seconds. (c) The twins drew more straight lines, to find the speed of the stick at various times when it is at various distances down stream.*

minutes, which is approximately at 75 meters from the stream's origin point."

Olivia was skeptical at first: "Would it matter if you took the time interval as $\delta t = 10$ seconds instead?" "Good point," said Oliver. "In fact, how about 5 or 1 or 1/100 second? The interval is supposed to be as tiny as we can imagine." So Olivia took over the drawing and made some additional lines on the graph. It turned out to be pretty hard to draw lines for small time intervals, but they did a few. The twins realized that their answers did vary, but only a little bit, as they tried to isolate the time of 4½ minutes more and more closely. They decided they were okay if they stuck with Oliver's original choice, $\delta t = 20$ seconds.

The twins looked for water speed at a few places along the stream. They drew lines for $t = 4$ minutes and 20 seconds (around 72 meters), 4 minutes and 40 seconds (around 80 meters), and so on (Figure 3.4c).

They got the slopes of these lines and equated them with the speed of the water at those locations along the stream. Ultimately, they made a table (Table 3.2) of the speed of the water at various points along the stream. Their conclusion was that the water is speeding up. An excited e-mail to the ecologist confirmed that

TABLE 3.2 Instantaneous Speed of the Water at Various Distances Along the Stream

DISTANCE ALONG STREAM (meters)	INSTANTANEOUS SPEED OF WATER (meters/sec)
72	0.22
75	0.33
80	0.47
84	0.56

they were right. This part of the stream bed turned out to run along a hillside, so that one would expect the speed of the water to increase.

ACCELERATION!

A real stick caught in a current and a real hiker on a twisting trail both experience a lot of speeding up and slowing down. Suppose someone parachutes out of a plane. When parachuting, at the moment of exiting the plane, the person speeds up. The speeding up diminishes as the parachutist approaches the terminal velocity, which is about 200 km/hour if he/she falls with arms and legs out. Then the chute pops open, and the speed decreases rapidly to a much lower value, just a couple of km/hour, as the parachutist falls to Earth. The parachutist's speed varies a lot over the duration of the jump. Another term for a changing speed is **acceleration**.

TAKING ABOUT PHYSICS: ACCELERATION

In physics, the word *acceleration* is used to refer to speeding up or slowing down. More generally, as we'll discuss in Chapter 4, it is also used to describe any deviation from uniform motion (that is, deviation from motion with one single instantaneous speed, in one single direction). In everyday speech on the other hand, we use *acceleration* to mean speeding up and *deceleration* to mean slowing down. (In this book, we will sometimes use the word *deceleration* when we mean slowing down, because it feels awkward to describe something coming to a stop as accelerating.)

DEFINING ACCELERATION

If in a small interval, Δt speed changes by an amount Δv, then

$$a_{ave} = \Delta v / \Delta t$$

This is the **average acceleration** (a_{ave})in that time interval. Also, just as we did in order to find instantaneous speed, we can imagine a limiting case where we consider a vanishingly short time interval, δt. Then we would find

$$a = \delta v/\delta t \tag{3.2}$$

which is called the *instantaneous acceleration*, or just *acceleration* for short.

In uniform acceleration, Equation 3.2 has the same value throughout the motion. The instantaneous and average acceleration are the same, $a_{ave} = a$, and they are a constant. It might help to compare and contrast the two concepts of uniform motion and uniform acceleration. In both, something is constant. For uniform motion, it is the speed. For uniform acceleration, it is the rate at which the speed changes, which is the acceleration. In uniform acceleration, speed changes in a uniform way, and the graph of speed versus time is a straight line. Instantaneous acceleration is equal to its average, and it is the slope of the line.

As an example of uniform acceleration, think about cliff diving, a sport in which athletes leap from cliffs as high as 30 meters (about as tall as a six-story building) and do various moves, such as somersaults and twists, on the way down. If a diver leaves the cliff and keeps his/her body sleek and aerodynamic (unlike the parachutist), he/she undergoes uniform acceleration all the way down. In Figure 3.5, the diver is contrasted with a parachutist who falls near the diver. At this point, the chute has been open for a long time. (Though the parachutist began her jump accelerating in the same way as the cliff diver, she ends her jump in uniform motion.)

Uniform acceleration is an important concept because it describes many common physical occurrences. Later, we shall show how the forces on an object cause it to accelerate. The simplest kind of force is one that stays constant throughout the motion of an object. A constant force makes the object accelerate with a constant acceleration.

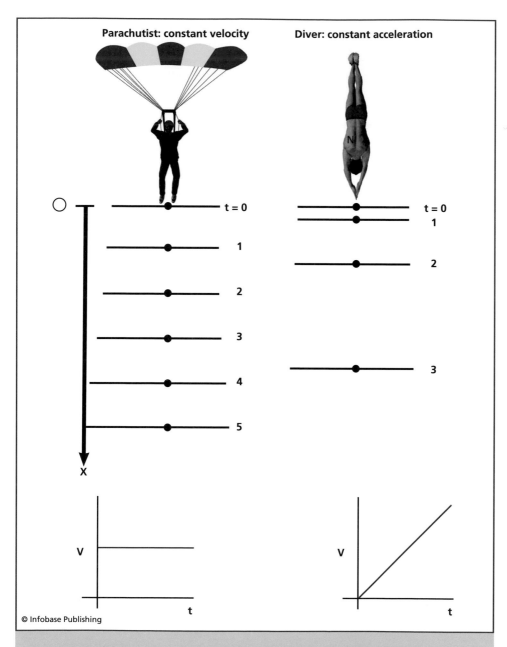

Figure 3.5 *The vertical positions of a parachutist and cliff diver, showing the difference between a motion with constant velocity and a motion with constant acceleration. The slope of the parachutist's v(t) line is zero, so the acceleration is zero. The uniform acceleration of the diver is just the slope of the v(t) line.*

THE UNITS OF ACCELERATION

What are the appropriate units to use to describe the amount of acceleration? The dimensions of acceleration are (length/time)/time = length/(time)^2. In SI system of units, speed is measured in m/sec. A speed that changes by 1 m/sec in a time of 1 sec would have an acceleration of 1 m/sec/sec or 1 m/sec^2. For example, the diver in Figure 3.5 increases his speed by 9.8 m/sec every second. Thus, his acceleration downward is 9.8 meters per second, per second, or 9.8 m/sec^2. Table 3.3 explores this and shows the different accelerations that you'd have if you were cliff diving on other planets.

OLIVER AND OLIVIA LOOK AT UNIFORM ACCELERATION

Oliver and Olivia watch several kids on bikes pass their house. One biker travels at a constant speed in a straight line, in uniform motion. The way Oliver would look at the motion would be to graph $x(t)$, as in Figure 3.6a. The graph of the bike's position, $x(t)$, makes a straight line, like that of the mice in Figure 3.2. The speed is the slope of the line. The way Olivia would describe motion would be to write the equation for the line as:

$$x(t) = vt + x_o$$

The slope of the line is v. The magnitude of v is the speed of the bike. The value x_o is the y-intercept and indicates where the object was at time $t = 0$.

On the other hand, another bike passes with uniform acceleration. It has a motion graph like in Figure 3.6b. This shape is a parabola. Olivia would write the equation for a parabola as:

$$x(t) = 1/2\ at^2 + v_o t + x_o \tag{3.3}$$

Cliff Diving on Other Planets

If you were cliff diving on Mars, how rapidly would you accelerate? How much time would you have to do a series of tricks designed to impress the judges? If you drop a pencil, an apple, or yourself toward the surface of a planet, the rate that you accelerate depends on the mass of the planet. (This rate also varies depending on how far away you are. If you are standing on Earth, you don't feel too much pull toward the surface of Mars!) Table 3.3 shows the rate of acceleration near the surface of various planets and our moon and sun. Also listed is the time it would take for you to fall 30 meters (approximately 6 floors of a building, a world-class, competitive cliff dive), disregarding atmospheric resistance.

TABLE 3.3	The Rate of Acceleration Near the Surface of Various Planets, Our Moon, and Our Sun	
NEAR THE SURFACE OF . . .	**YOUR ACCELERATION WOULD BE . . . (m/s²)**	**TIME IT WOULD TAKE YOU TO FALL 30 METERS (Seconds)**
Mercury	3.7	4.0
Venus	8.9	2.6
Earth	9.8	2.5
Mars	3.7	4.0
Jupiter	25	1.5
Saturn	10.4	2.4
Sun	275	0.5
Moon	1.6	6.1

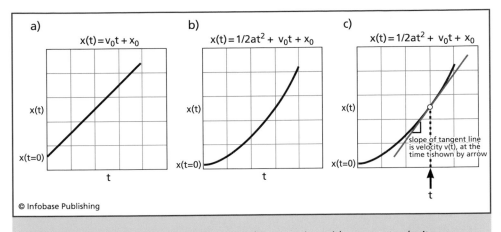

Figure 3.6 *(a) The position graph of an object moving with constant velocity. (b) The position graph of an object moving with constant acceleration. (c) Drawing the tangent line for one time (t) on a position graph will give you the instantaneous velocity. The slope of the line is v(t) = at + v_0, the instantaneous velocity at that time.*

The larger a is, the more curved the parabola is. It turns out that

$$v(t) = at + v_o \qquad (3.4)$$

is the speed of the bike at any time (t). At time $t = 0$ the speed is v_o. The acceleration (a) is the slope of the $v(t)$ line given in Equation 3.4. Equations 3.3 and 3.4 are very important in kinematics.

You might be wondering what happened to the old rule about speed being the slope of a position graph. Does Equation 3.4 mean that it won't work anymore? In fact it does. But in a situation of acceleration, the graph of $x(t)$ is not a straight line. To find the speed at a time t, we find the slope of the line tangent to the graph at time t. If acceleration is zero, then the slope of Equation 3.4 is v_o, a constant. The speed has that value for all time.

This is what the twins did when they analyzed the stick in the stream. Their lines did a decent job of approximating the tangent line, whose slope was $v(t)$ (Figure 3.6c). In the case of uniform acceleration, $v(t)$ is given by Equation 3.4.

CONCLUSION: PICTURES VERSUS WORDS

"Five!" shout Oliver and Olivia, at almost the same moment. This is the time at which Oliver's curves for mouse and jaguar motion crossed, as you saw in Figure 3.4. It is also the solution to Olivia's equation, $t^2 - 10 = 3t$, which could be rewritten as

$$t^2 - 3t - 10 = 0,$$

which factors to

$$(t - 5)(t + 2) = 0$$

The fact that there is also a solution $t = -2$ sec bothered Olivia for a moment. She realized that the mouse and jaguar could not have met at $t = -2$ sec because the animals hadn't started running until $t = 0$. "Oh well," she thought, "math gives us extra solutions that don't fit with physical situations." In the real, physical world, the past determines the future and gives us only one, real way things can happen. She looked enviously at Oliver's graph, which gives only the one solution. But wait, if she continued his graph to the negative times as in Figure 3.7, then a second solution shows up! It is not right for the physics problem, but it's there in the math when the graphs are drawn for all times, not just for times greater than zero.

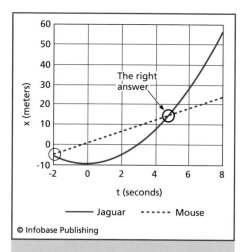

© Infobase Publishing

Figure 3.7 *Olivia and Oliver's graph of position (x) versus time (t) for the mouse and the jaguar. The graph of Figure 3.1 has been extended to times less than t = 0. The circled points on the graph show where the curves cross. The one at t = 5 seconds is the right answer to the problem.*

Oliver smiled at his sister's addition to his graph. They then both went to work on the extra-credit problem, which was pretty easy when they used Equation 3.4 in this chapter. The mouse has $a = 0$, $v_o = 3$, and $x_o = 0$, so its speed is $v_o = 3$ m/sec at all times. The jaguar has $a = 2$, $v_o = 0$, and $x_o = -10$, so its speed is $2t = 10$ m/sec at the time $t = 5$ seconds. Their physics teacher, Dr. Kelp, is pleased with their work. Oliver and Olivia are pleased too, not just to get another couple of right answers, but to realize that the way they thought about physics is not so different after all.

CHAPTER 4

Motion in a Three-Dimensional World: Using Vectors to Describe Kinematics

TOM FOUGHT TO PUT THE NOSE OF HIS PLANE INTO THE WIND in order to make the tricky takeoff, rejoin his squadron, and complete the mission. Pilots always take off heading straight into the wind, for maximum stability. But on this gray day, the wind was unreliable. It had shifted suddenly, so it was blowing from 40° west of north. He needed to adjust quickly. Did he under- or over-correct the direction of the plane's motion? He couldn't tell as another blast of wind sent the plane skidding; and then the plane was rolling over. Tom realized how bad it was. He might not survive the crash. Noise and flames erupted simultaneously. It would only take a few seconds for it all to be over. As it happened, he closed his eyes, and waited.

Slowly, he opened his eyes. "Retry or Quit?" were his options. He selected "Quit." This game was surprisingly hard; at this rate he was never going to succeed on the mission and beat this level.

Part of the problem was that he was playing the game from a computer keyboard. In order to pick the direction of motion of the plane, he had to use the arrow keys. Hitting the *left arrow-key* gave him speed to the west, and the *up-arrow key* gave him speed to the north. More hits on an arrow made him go faster in the direction of the arrow.

Tom's challenge was to find the combination of arrows he was supposed to hit in order to take off in a certain, precise direction. Just going on instinct was evidently not enough to meet the challenge. In physics class, Tom was just getting to the idea of motion in two and three dimensions. His teacher had just extended the idea of speed to velocity, which means speed in a certain direction. Tom wondered if there was something about velocity in his physics book that would teach him how to use the arrow keys on his computer keyboard to pick the right velocity for the plane.

In this chapter, we will work with the idea that displacement, velocity, and acceleration are vectors. Knowing how to do physics with vectors allows us to understand how velocity and acceleration are related in real-world situations.

LIFE IN LINELAND

In the book *Flatland: A Romance of Many Dimensions*, by Edwin A. Abbott, there is a realm called Lineland, where the creatures are little line segments (male) or points (female).[9] They are only able to move back and forth along a single, straight line. The Lineland folks could not dream of even two dimensions, like a flat sheet of paper, much less imagine the third dimension which is the world we live in.

As limited as they are, Linelanders would still understand the concepts of displacement, speed, and acceleration, as we talked about them in Chapters 2 and 3. They could move a certain distance from a reference position—a **displacement**. Linelanders would have a well-defined instantaneous speed and acceleration at every moment. They would also know that these quantities have a direction, which are indicated with signs, either positive or negative. Linelanders would be mindful of the signs when they use the kinematic equations in Chapter 3. Speed and acceleration would either be to the left (negative) or to the right (positive). We will begin by giving an example of kinematics in one-dimensional Lineland. But motion in two and higher dimensions, like Tom's takeoff, will need more than a + or − sign to describe its direction. In order to do this, we introduce and explore the concept of vectors.

GETTING THE SIGNS RIGHT

What does it mean when the velocity of a Lineland resident is negative or positive? She is moving left when it is negative, and right when it is positive. Suppose that a woman of Lineland begins at position $x_o = -5$ cm, with an initial speed of $v_o = 0$, and accelerates with $a = -2$ cm/ sec^2. She is in a hurry to meet a friend toward her left side, located at position −14 cm as in Figure 4.1a. What are her displacement and speed at later times; and in particular, at what time will she run into her friend and how fast will she be moving when they collide? (These questions are like the jaguar and mouse problem in Chapter 3.) We use $x(t) = 1/2 \, at^2 + v_o t + x_o$ as in Equation 3.3. The woman accelerates to the left, which is why her acceleration has a negative sign: $a < 0$. The woman will be at a position

$$x(t) = (-t^2 - 5) \text{ cm}$$

at a time of t seconds. When $t = 3$ sec, she will run into the friend, because

$$x(3) = (-3^2 - 5) \text{ cm} = -14 \text{ cm}$$

The woman's speed at time t is $v(t) = at + v_o = -2t$ as in Equation 3.4. She is speeding up constantly, moving left. At $t = 3$ sec, when she runs into her friend her speed is −6 cm/sec. (Hopefully, her friend forgives her for the collision. This happens a lot in Lineland.) Now suppose the woman has a Lineland husband who begins at position $x_o = -4$ cm.

He is also moving with $a = -2$ cm/sec², and his initial speed is $v_o = 4$ cm/sec. Though initially he is moving to the right at 4 cm/sec, the negative sign on his acceleration shows that is is directed to the left. He is slowing down in order to turn around and reach his wife. If he keeps on this way, there will be a time, $t = 2$ sec, when his speed is zero and he has stopped. After that, he begins picking up speed again, moving to the left. (Will he get to his wife before the time of the collision? No. He would need to accelerate at a rate faster than hers in order to overtake her at all.) Figures 4.1a and 4.1b show this series of events.

In summary, in one dimension, the sign of speed tells you which way a body is moving. The sign of acceleration describes whether it is speeding up or slowing down based on the following: If the sign of velocity and acceleration agree, the object is speeding up. If the sign of velocity and acceleration disagree, the object is slowing down.

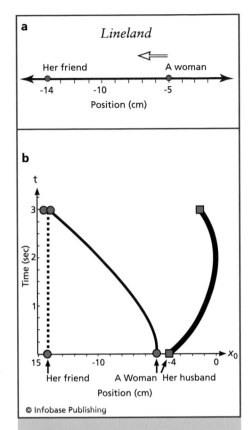

Figure 4.1 *(a) A Lineland woman moves in the direction toward her stationary friend. (b) The woman collides with her friend, but her husband does not catch up to them.*

BEYOND LINELAND: KINEMATIC QUANTITIES AS VECTORS

Consider the hiker we talked about in Chapter 3. If a hiker follows a trail to a waterfall, his steps of size δd always point along

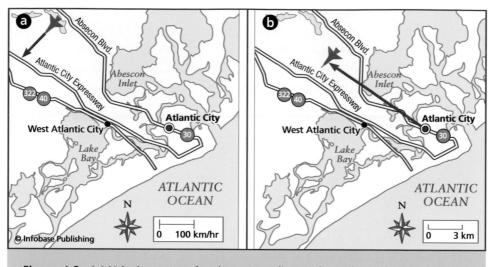

Figure 4.2 *(a) Velocity vector of a plane: According to the scale marker, the length of this vector indicates its speed is around 100 km/hr. (b) Displacement vector of a plane: According to the scale marker, its position is around 10 km outside of Atlantic City, N.J.*

the trail. We need a way to talk about kinematic and dynamic quantities like this, with not only a size, but also a direction in which they point. Such quantities are known as **vectors**. A displacement of "5 miles, North" is a vector. So is the acceleration "9.8 m/s², downward." Vectors can be described in words like these, by writing formulas, or by drawing them as arrows whose length represents their size and point in the direction needed. When we want to write a formula that describes vectors, we write the name of the vector in boldface. Thus, *d* would stand for a displacement vector, and we would say "*d* = 5 miles, North" or "The hiker just took a step, δ*d* = 20 cm, Northwest" or "*a* = 9.8 m/s² downward."

Figure 4.2 shows vector quantities related to a plane in flight. Some new use of language accompanies the new way to talk about kinematic quantities as vectors. The words *displacement* and *acceleration* will now indicate vector quantities. (Sometimes people will even use the phrase *displacement vector* to get the idea across.) As it happens though, the word *speed* is never used in physics to mean a vector. While we would say that the plane of Figure 4.2a is moving with a speed of 100 km/hr, we would say that "100 km/hr, Southwest" is the plane's velocity vector. In other words, velocity is the vector quantity that generalizes the non-vector idea of speed.

Consider the hiker in Figure 4.3. The arrows are meant to represent her velocity vector at various times. An object's velocity vector is always tangent to its path. Moreover, the lengths of the arrows in Figure 4.3 give us speed information. The practice of drawing a vector with its length proportional to the size of the quantity lets us, with one symbol, convey both speed and directional information about the hiker's motion.

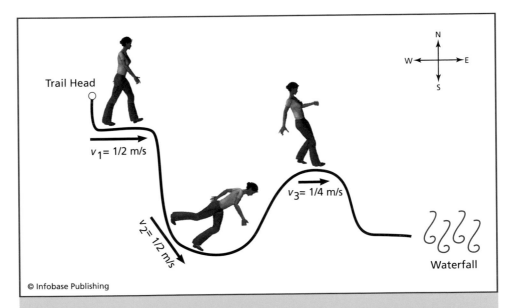

Figure 4.3 *The velocity vector of a hiker, drawn at various points during the hike. Not only does the direction of the vector tell you which way she is moving, but the length of the vector tells you how fast the hiker is going.*

THE ANATOMY OF A VECTOR

As seen in Figures 4.2 and 4.3, a vector has a fairly simple structure. It has a "tip" and a "tail." To use vectors in physics, we need to distinguish the tip from the tail. In Figure 4.4a, there are two vectors that differ only in that their tip and tail positions are reversed. These two are not the same vector, but are in fact opposites. If these were meant to show you the velocities of flying planes, one orientation (the vector V) might mean that the velocity is pointing south, and the other (the vector $-V$) pointing north. A vector is considered to have the same meaning no matter where it is drawn on paper. We could draw three velocity vectors for three different airplanes, v_1, v_2, and v_3, as in Figure 4.4b. A drawing like this might help us if we are wondering how their directions of motion relate to each other; say, if any two planes are traveling in the same direction or at right angles to each other (v_2 and v_3 look like they are pretty much at right angles). We can redraw those same three vectors in many correct ways, as indicated in Figure 4.4c. The pictures that are drawn with several vectors, tip-to-tail, one after the other, turn out to be a useful way to represent the sum of a bunch of vector quantities. Also, calculations involving the difference between two vector quantities can be usefully done by drawing two vectors tail-to-tail. We will return to these topics later.

TALKING ABOUT PHYSICS: VECTORS AND SCALARS

Suppose an object moves at constant speed (v) over a time (t). The idea that it covers a distance (d) with $d = vt$ is an algebraic equation we considered in Chapter 2. The three symbols, d, v, and t represent non-vectors. Vectors are so common in physics that non-vectors have their own name—**scalars**. Time, mass, temperature, and energy are other scalars in physics.

As we've mentioned, one way to indicate that a quantity is a vector is to use a bold symbol, for example, using v to mean a velocity vector. If we want to talk about the size of v, we can go back

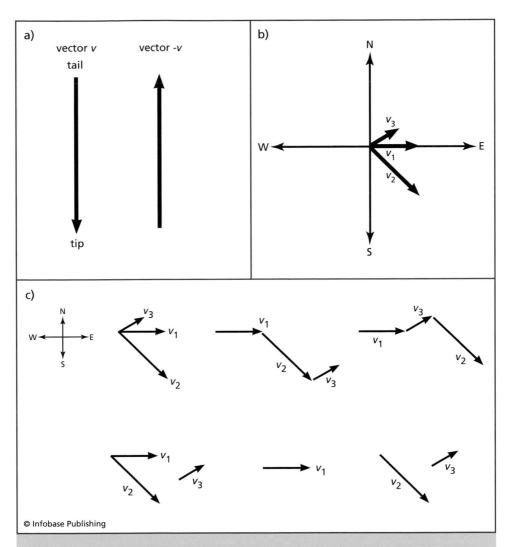

Figure 4.4 *(a) The anatomy of a vector: The direction is the way that the tip is pointing; reverse the tip and tail of a vector* **V** *and you get the opposite of the vector, written as* −**V**. *(b) Three vectors,* **v**$_1$, **v**$_2$, *and* **v**$_3$: *When we draw them like this, with their tails all located at the same origin, it helps us see how their directions relate to each other. (c) Many correct ways to draw the same set of vectors: We only need to keep their lengths and directions the same.*

to using the symbol (v). We have a choice of calling the symbol that is not in bold either the "size of the velocity" or the "speed." Thus, every vector has a scalar quantity associated with it: its size. Speed is a scalar quantity. It is also the size of the velocity vector. The equation $d = vt$ refers to scalar quantities. It is a true equation, but it is also true and more general to say $d = vt$, meaning that the displacement and average velocity vector point in the same direction and they are related by the time. The meaning of a vector multiplied by a scalar like "vt" is discussed in Rule 2 in the next section.

There are many good ways to talk about the direction of a vector, as shown in Figure 4.5a. One valid way is to say: "Look at that vector A drawn on my paper; its direction is obvious!" A second way is to use some nearby reference points, like the directions of the compass located near the vector and say: "A points directly northeast." A third way is again to have a reference, like the x-y axes and say: "Look at the x-y axes, and you'll see that A points at 45° above the horizontal, x axis, while the vector B points at 10° below the x axis." This last way has clear advantages if we have a direction that isn't, for example, purely north or northeast. There is a fourth way that we'll describe in the next section. It is finding how many steps along the x and y axes you would need to take to end up pointing in the direction of the vector. (This way holds the key to Tom's problem.)

VECTOR ALGEBRA

The following are two basic rules for doing algebra with vectors—ones that will allow us to write equations and get full understanding of how things move in two or three dimensions.

Rule 1: Vectors Add to Form New Vectors

Any vector can be written as the sum of other vectors. We add vectors by drawing them tip to tail. Their sum is drawn from the tail of the first vector to the tip of the second. So Figure 4.5b represents the cases that $a = b + c$ and also $a = e + f$.

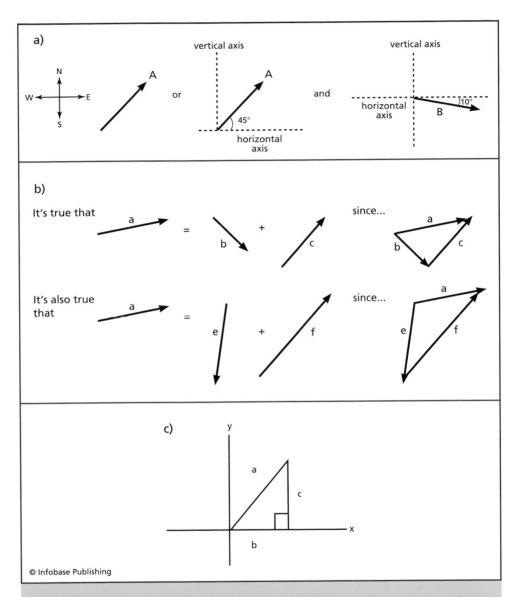

Figure 4.5 *(a) You can draw the direction of a vector, draw it against some coordinate axes, or draw it and show the angle it makes with one of those axes. (b) Vectors can be added to make new vectors. Any vector **(a)** can be broken down into two (or more) other vectors that together add up to **a**. (c) A very convenient way to break down any vector like **a** involves choosing coordinate axes and finding two vectors, one **(b)** along the horizontal axis and one **(c)** along the vertical, that add up to **a**.*

Rule 1, which lets Tom solve his problem, is called "breaking the vector into components." That is, one finds two vectors, *b* and *c,* that sum to *a*, and strategically picks *b* and *c* to be at right angles, parallel to whatever *x*, *y* coordinate axes are convenient, say, as in Figure 4.5c. Then, the vector *a* lies along the hypotenuse of a right triangle with legs of length *b* and *c*. With Rule 1 about vector addition, you can give a perfect description of the vector *a* in a number of ways. For example: "*a* can be drawn with its tail at the origin $(x,y) = (0,0)$ and its head at the point (b,c)" or "*a* lies along the hypotenuse of a triangle with horizontal leg of length *b* and vertical of length *c*" or "*a* makes an angle θ with the horizontal axis so that $\tan(\theta) = c/b$ and *a*'s length is $a = \sqrt{b^2 + c^2}$.

There are two reasons why doing algebra with vectors is important. The first reason is mathematical convenience. You can think of, and write, a vector in terms of its components in any formula because they are "identical" from a mathematical point of view. Second, real-world vector quantities often add up to a new vector with a real-world meaning. Consider the runners who make a relay team, as they do every four years when the Summer Olympic Games are held, to carry a torch from a starting point to an ending point in the Olympic stadium.[10] The first runner's displacement from his origin is d_1, the displacement of the second runner from where he picked up the torch is d_2, and so on to the Nth runner (Figure 4.6). (In the case of the 2004 Olympic Games, N was around 3,600.) The meaning of the sum of vectors is the total displacement of the torch from its starting point:

$$d = d_1 + d_2 + \ldots = \sum_{i=1}^{N} d_i$$

Though the torch made its way all over the world in the summer of 2004, the actual displacement *d* was not very great in size; it started in the city of ancient Olympia and ended up in Athens, both of which are in the country of Greece.

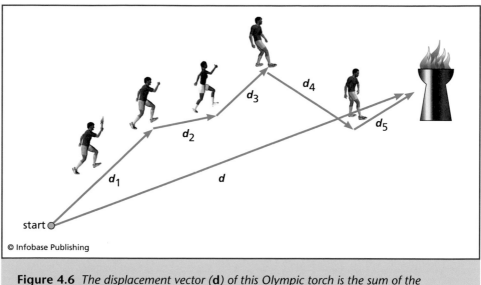

Figure 4.6 *The displacement vector (**d**) of this Olympic torch is the sum of the displacement vectors of the five runners who handed it off to each other in the torch relay.*

Rule 2: Vectors Can Be Multiplied by a Scalar to Form a New Vector

Suppose you are asked to draw the velocity vectors for two planes, one going at v_1 = 100 km/hr, Southwest and the second at v_2 = 200 km/hr, Southwest. These two vectors have a relationship which can be written as:

$$v_2 = 2v_1$$

We are saying that $2v_1$ denotes a vector in the same direction as v_1, and with twice the size. One could just as well write v_1 = $(0.5)v_2$, which says that v_1 has half the size of v_2. You can multiply a vector by any positive real number, w. The new vector wV has a length which is w times the length of the vector V, and it points in exactly the same direction.

What about using negative real numbers? That too is possible, and it relates to our claim (see Figure 4.4a) that the vector $-V$ looked like V, but is its "opposite." Multiplying a vector by a negative number, $-w$, will produce a new vector pointed in the opposite direction, as well as one with a length that is different by the factor w.

With Rules 1 and 2, we can talk about the difference of two vectors. Just as we can write

$$p - q = p + (-q)$$

for the scalar quantities p and q; we can write that for the vectors A and B:

$$A - B = A + (-B)$$

The vector C is the difference of A and B. We have a choice. We can get C by drawing A and B tail-to-tail and then connecting their heads. Figure 4.7 illustrates this. We can also use B to draw $-B$ and then get C by drawing A and $-B$ tip-to-tail and connecting the tail of A with the tip of B, in the usual way we would add two vectors.

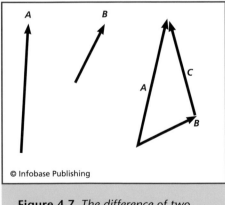

© Infobase Publishing

Figure 4.7 *The difference of two vectors: $C = A - B$.*

The difference of vectors shows up in many places. The difference between the horse's displacement vectors, d_o and d_1 in Figure 4.8b in the next section, is itself a displacement vector called δd_1. The relative velocity of two objects, which we will explore in Chapter 7, is the difference between two velocity vectors. For example, if according to you, Tom is flying at velocity v_{Tom} and a bird is flying near him with speed v_{Bird}, then Tom sees the bird relative to himself at a velocity $v = v_{Bird} - v_{Tom}$.

UNIFORM AND NON-UNIFORM MOTION WITH VECTORS

Suppose a horse gallops across a meadow at constant speed, moving due east. His velocity vector is v. The displacement vector in time t has size vt and direction east. Using the language of vectors, we'd say:

$$d = vt$$

Let's say the horse gallops at $v = 3$ furlongs/minute east for $t = 10$ seconds (1 furlong = 220 yards). The horse's displacement vector over that time is

$$d = (3 \text{ furlongs/min})(10 \text{ secs})(1 \text{ min/60 sec}) \text{ east}$$
$$= 0.5 \text{ furlongs east}$$

This new language of vectors was not necessary for the horse above. Such a calculation could be done for a Lincland horse using only scalars, since the motion is in a straight line. But suppose that, as in Figure 4.8a, the horse is startled at time $t = t_1$ by some wolves in a field. He turns abruptly to race north for another time $t = t_2$ until he tires and stops. The turn takes a very brief time, Δt. The displacement over his whole motion is the sum of the little vectors that make up his motion, like the Olympic torch example in Figure 4.6. His net displacement, d, is the sum of $A = vt_1$ east, $B = vt_2$ north:

$$d = A + B$$

The horse's displacement has a size $d = \sqrt{(vt_1)^2 + (vt_2)^2} = v\sqrt{t_1^2 + t_2^2}$. He has gone less far than if he'd kept running in a straight line for the total time $t_1 + t_2$.

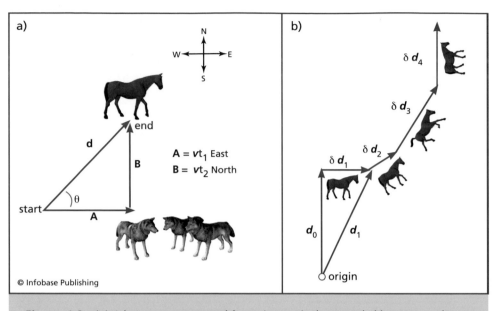

Figure 4.8 *(a) A horse runs eastward for a time t_1, is then startled by some wolves. The horse races northward for a time t_2. (b) Details of the position of the horse as it veers from east to north. In four successive short time intervals, δt, its displacement vectors change by the four different vectors $\delta d_1 - \delta d_4$.*

Let's put in numbers to see how these formulas would work in a real problem. Suppose $v = 3$ furlongs/minute, t_1 is 1/4 minute and t_2 is 1/3 minute. What are d, the length of the hypotenuse, and the angle θ in Figure 4.8a? Doing the math, d = 5/4 furlongs = 1.25 furlongs. If the horse had run in a straight line, the distance would be d = (3) (1/4 + 1/3) = 1.75 furlongs. The angle θ has a tangent of 4/3, which makes θ approximately 53°.

Now consider the panicky horse's velocity. It starts out pointing east and ends up pointing north. In between times, it must be pointing somewhere in between. We can find both its size and direction at every instant with the vector equation

$$v = \delta d / \delta t$$

This equation resembles the one for instantaneous speed from Chapter 3. Figure 4.8b is a close-up of the horse's motion before, during, and after he veers northward, as observed by his owner standing at the origin. The owner sees him displaced by a vector d_0 at time 0, d_1 after a time δt, and so on. In each of four tiny time intervals of size δt, his speed relates to the distance he has gone as $v = \delta d / \delta t$. Thus, he has slowed down in the second time interval, sped up in the third, and slowed back to his original speed in the fourth. In order of size, his speeds are $v_3 > v_4 > v_1 > v_2$. In each time interval, his velocity vector is parallel to the change in his displacement vector from the origin:

$$\mathbf{v}_i \parallel \delta \mathbf{d}_i \text{ where } i = 1, 2, 3, \text{ or } 4$$

His motion points in these directions during the four successive time intervals of size δt:

Direction	Time interval
East	1st
30° north of east	2nd
60° north of east	3rd
North	4th

Any velocity vector, $\mathbf{v}_i$ where the instantaneous velocity vector doesn't stay the same—either the same in length or the same in direction, or both (as in the case of this horse)—is a motion where there is acceleration. We can detect acceleration when we analyze a motion by looking for a change in the velocity vector's size, direction, or both. It would take a good rider to stay in the saddle during the horse's time of acceleration. As you may know from riding in a car that takes a corner very quickly or starts up from a red light very abruptly, the shorter the time it takes to change velocity, the larger the acceleration and the more jolting it is for the rider. The jolting is due to **forces**. As we'll discuss in Chapters 6 and 7, forces and accelerations go hand in hand. In the math below, we see how acceleration relates to the rapidity of the change in velocity.

BUILD AN ACCELEROMETER

You can easily create an accelerometer, an instrument that detects when your motion is accelerated (Figure 4.9a). Suspend a small object, like a key or small piece of clay, from a string. Tape or tie the end of the string to the lid of an empty, see-through jar. Or if you are in a situation where it is okay to have an open flame, a lit candle inside a jar will also act as an accelerometer. The hanging object or the flame acts as an indicator of acceleration.

If you move in a uniform way (try to move smoothly with the same speed, same direction) while holding the accelerometer, the bob will hang straight down (or candle flame will burn straight up). When you change direction and/or change speed, the indicator will do something else. You can walk or run with your invention, or take it into the car and see what it does when someone is driving. Figure 4.9b shows a person holding an accelerometer who is increasing the speed of his motion. It turns out that the indicator is displaced in a direction that is opposite to that of the acceleration. Why opposite? We will discover why in Chapter 6, when we make the connection between acceleration and force. Figure 4.9c shows a different accelerated motion. The person spins in a circle, holding an accelerometer out straight ahead with his arms outstretched. (Try this if you have constructed your own accelerometer.) What does the displacement of the indicator (outward, away from the center of the circle) mean about the direction of the acceleration of the arms and hands that hold the accelerometer? (Answer: They are accelerating inward, toward the center of the circle.)

FINDING THE ACCELERATION VECTOR

For one-dimensional motion in Chapter 3, we saw that acceleration happens when there is a change in an object's speed, Δv. For any small time interval Δt, the average acceleration during that time, a_{ave}, obeyed $a_{ave} = \Delta v/\Delta t$. In the idealized case where we measured the velocity change (δv) during a very small time in-

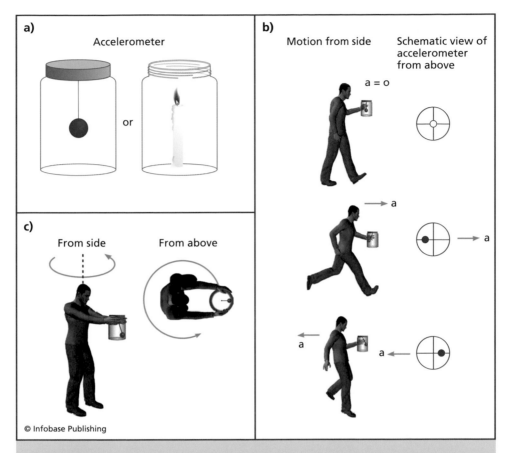

Figure 4.9 *(a) An accelerometer can consist of an indicator, like a small object suspended from a string or the flame of a candle. (b) The indicator of an accelerometer moves in a way that is* opposite *to the direction of the acceleration. (c) Someone moves in a circle holding an accelerometer. The indicator moves outward, indicating that its acceleration is inward, toward the center.*

terval, δ*t*, the acceleration being described was the instantaneous acceleration (*a*) and it was defined as *a* = δ*v*/δ*t*.

Just as we did when we analyzed the displacement of the galloping horse, we claim that the old kinematic equations are scalar versions of vector equations. The old versions are fine for a one-dimensional motion, but we need the vector versions to describe motion in the three-dimensional real world.

In the limit of a tiny time interval δt, during which the velocity vector changes by the fantastically tiny amount δv:

$$a = \delta v/\delta t$$

This defines the instantaneous acceleration vector **a**. If the time interval Δt is not so small, we are calculating an average acceleration over that time interval:

$$a_{ave} = \Delta v/\Delta t$$

Figure 4.10 illustrates this for a skateboarding move known as an "ollie." You can ollie either standing still or rolling forward. The figure shows a skateboarder rolling with velocity v_1 in the forward direction. The skateboarder is going to accelerate. To get the necessary force, he bends his knees, slams his back foot down on the tail of the skateboard and jumps into the air off of his back foot. All this has to happen in a smooth, quick set of motions. Suppose that the entire sequence takes a time, Δt, and the skateboarder ends up as in the second picture, with a velocity v_2. The skateboarder's acceleration is in the time interval of the ollie is

$$a_{ave} = \Delta v/\Delta t = (v_2 - v_1)/\Delta t$$

The acceleration vector (a_{ave}) points upward and backward, as is sketched out in Figure 4.10.

Again, we have an equation involving vectors (acceleration and velocity) where we encountered scalar versions before (in Chapter 3). The scalar versions say that the *size* of the velocity change is the size of the acceleration, multiplied by time. The vector version agrees and gives us the additional insight that the *direction* of the velocity change equals the direction of the acceleration. It seems simple, but when this equation was introduced into Tom's physics class, confusion broke out. One student said that the new, vector equation created a paradox. (A paradox is statement that seems to contradict itself and/or common sense.) That is, $\delta \boldsymbol{v} = \boldsymbol{a}\delta t$ was supposed to be an extension of the old scalar equation, $\delta v = a\delta t$. But, the student observed, when you hold your accelerometer out and spin in a circle, moving at an even, uniform speed, the object has $\delta v = 0$. The old equation would predict that $a = 0$, that there is no acceleration. But the new vector equation would predict there is acceleration. One of these conclusions has to be wrong. An accelerometer is either going to tell you that the acceleration is zero or not!

Figure 4.10 *The difference in the skateboarder's velocity vector, Δv, divided by the time interval, Δt, gives the skater's acceleration, a_{ave}, while performing the move.*

This stumped a lot of people, including Tom, but Dr. Kelp had a good answer. The key idea is that the velocity changes direction between time t and time $t + \delta t$. Thus, $\delta \boldsymbol{v}$ is the difference between those two differently directed velocity vectors. Its size is δv, which is not zero. So there *is* an acceleration. The lesson to be learned, said Dr. Kelp, is that you have to be careful about interpreting symbols in scalar equations like $\delta v = a\delta t$. You have to remember that to find δv, you find the vector ($\delta \boldsymbol{v}$) which is the difference between two velocity vectors. Then afterward you find its size, δv. You can't skip the step of treating velocity like a vector and just take the difference between the speeds at those two times. Only if those two velocities were parallel to each other as well as being the same size would it be true that $\delta v = 0$.

As we've implied before, acceleration comes from forces. The action of slamming the back foot down on the tail of the skateboard creates a force that catapults the board and the skateboarder's body upward and backward. Additional upward acceleration of the skateboarder's body comes from the skateboarder springing up from a crouch, just like jumping up from solid ground.

CONCLUSION: TAKING OFF INTO THE WIND

Tom realized that he could use Rule 1 about addition of velocity vectors to come up with a vector pointing 40° west of north. Tom sketched out vector, **V**, and then thought about the components **A** and **B** that would add up to **V**. The length of **V** wasn't too important (even one tap seemed to give enough speed to get airborne) but the direction was. The direction was given by θ where

$$\tan \theta = \tan (40°) = 0.8391$$

(Tom used his calculator to find this.) In other words, the ratio of the speed west, **B**, to the speed north, **A**, needed to be approximately

$$B/A = 0.8391$$

What **A** and **B** should he pick? There wasn't a perfect answer involving only a few taps on the arrow keys. But the ratio **B/A** = 5/6 = 0.8333 seemed pretty close. If he gave the plane 6 key taps of speed north, and 5 key taps of speed west, it might be good enough. It turned out that it was, and Tom was able to take off without disaster.

As Tom's plane climbed and began to turn to search for his squadron, he noticed that other ideas from his physics class were falling into place. For example, the accelerometer on his plane's control panel registered not only when he changed speed, but also when he changed his direction of motion. As he made a large circle in order to search for his squadron, his accelerometer indicated an acceleration toward the center of the circle, like the spinning person in Figure 4.9. It all made sense. Tom was able to complete his mission. The world was safe once more, thanks to Tom and to physics.

CHAPTER 5

Accelerated Motions

Every year, Lori's physics class votes on where to take their end-of-the-year trip. Euclid Beach Park has won every year; it even won when Lori's dad took physics at the same school! They always seem to have a new roller coaster, but even the old ones from her dad's time are worth riding.

Lori and her friends have an ongoing debate about where to sit in the car in order to get the most g-forces. High g-forces give you a heavy feeling and are strong when you are rounding a curve or valley. These alternate with the floating, weightless feeling of low g-forces, when you are descending a huge drop. Lori and her friends are not sure where g-forces come from. Do they have anything to do with the kinds of forces they are beginning to study in physics? Whatever they are, they make the ride exciting!

Dr. Kelp explains g-forces are defined as $g - a$, where g is the acceleration of gravity, and a is the acceleration of your body. So when you accelerate upward, g-forces are strong, because g and $-a$ are parallel. When you are in **free fall** like a cliff diver, g-forces vanish, because $g = a$.

In this chapter, we work on finding the acceleration vectors for various real-world motions, like passengers on a plane or an amusement park ride.

CIRCULAR MOTION: DO BUGS GET DIZZY?

Motion in a circle at constant speed is a common situation in physics.[11] In Figure 5.1a, a bug undergoes such motion as it clings to the tip of the second hand of a clock. We see vectors for its displacement from the center and for its velocity. When the hand points to 12:00, the bug is moving to the right. When it points to 3:00, the bug is moving downward, and so on. The two important features of a circular motion are the radius of the circle (here, the length of the second hand) and the time period (here, one minute). The second hand is a concrete version of the bug's ever-changing displacement vector from the center of the circle. Its velocity and acceleration vectors are also changing, and it is these qualities that we intend to find in this section.

The bug's displacement vector from the clock center (the second hand) will rotate just a tiny bit in a very short time of, say, δt. This change in position vector is δd, as shown in Figure 5.1b. From our discussion in Chapter 4, we expect this change to be related to the velocity as $v = \delta d/\delta t$. (The velocity shown in Figure 5.1b is labeled $v_{12:00}$ in Figure 5.1a.) From this relationship, which is true for any motion, we know that instantaneous change in position is parallel to velocity. However, there is some additional interesting geometry that is specific to circular motion. From picture 5.1b we see that δd, and therefore v, is perpendicular to d at every moment.

Thus, for circular motion, the velocity (v) points along the circumference, at right angles to d (which we might have known from common sense, as in Figure 5.1a). But we can use similar reasoning to figure out something less obvious. As we discussed in Chapter 4, acceleration is defined from change in velocity as $a = \delta v/\delta t$. Figure 5.1c shows what happens to the velocity vector during δt. From this picture we see that δv, and therefore the acceleration, a, is perpendicular to v at every moment.

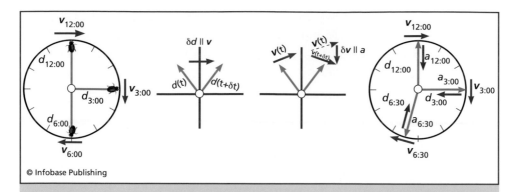

© Infobase Publishing

Figure 5.1 *(a) A bug riding on a second hand has displacement and velocity vectors that, at every moment, are perpendicular to each other. (b) The change in the bug's position vector over a tiny time interval. (c) The corresponding change in the bug's velocity vector. (d) The position, velocity, and acceleration vectors of the bug at various times.*

Figure 5.1d indicates how the displacement, velocity, and acceleration vectors rotate in a circle. Displacement points outward, velocity along the circumference, and acceleration inward, which was something we stated in Chapter 4 for the spinning person holding his accelerometer. This line of reasoning not only gives the directions of these vectors, but also lets us find the sizes of the velocity and acceleration. Remember that all of these vectors finish one complete rotation in one time period, which we will call *T*. So the speed (*v*) is the length of the circumference of the circle divided by the time:

v = circumference/time = 2π (radius of circle traced by d)/T

Let's give the symbol R to the radius of the circle traced out by *d*. Then,

$$v = 2\pi R/T \qquad (5.1)$$

This equation predicts that the bug's speed is proportional to how far out on the hand it is clinging. If the hand were R = 15 cm in length, the bug's speed would be $v = 2\pi$ (15 cm)/(60 sec) = π/2 cm/sec = 1.57 cm/sec. If a second bug were clinging halfway along the hand, it would cover half the distance in a minute that the first bug covers. It would only be moving at half the speed of the first bug, or around 0.79 cm/sec. To see this principle in action, you can do the following experiment: Put two pennies on a tabletop and touching the edge of a ruler. One should be twice as far from the end of the ruler as the other. Hold that end of the ruler down with your thumb. Give the free end of the ruler a shove so that the pennies are launched by the ruler. The one that is farther from the end will go faster. In fact, the penny that is two times as far from the center of rotation should fly away going two times as fast. (How can you tell it goes exactly twice as fast? See Robert Ehrlich's book *The Cosmological Milkshake* for one way.[12])

We can apply the idea we just used to find the size of the acceleration. That is, the mathematical relationship between v, d, and time is identical to the relationship between a, v, and time, only the names of the symbols are different:

$$v = \delta d / \delta t \text{ and } a = \delta v / \delta t$$

Also identical is the fact that for **uniform circular motion**, both displacement (d) and velocity (v) rotate in a circle. The radius of the displacement circle is the size of the displacement vector (which we have called R). Similarly, the radius of the velocity circle is the size of the velocity vector (v). We conclude that the size of the acceleration must be equal to the circumference of the circle traced out by the velocity vector, divided by the time:

$$a = 2\pi v / T$$

Substituting in for v from Equation 5.1, the acceleration is

$$a = R(2\pi/T)^2 \tag{5.2}$$

Acceleration grows with radius, so a bug clinging halfway along the hand would not only have half the speed, but also half the acceleration of a bug at the tip. Also, acceleration increases by $1/T^2$. A bug that grabs onto the minute hand instead of the second hand of a clock would have a period (T), which is 60 times as long. This translates into an acceleration which is 1/3600 times as great.

Equations 5.1 and 5.2 describe any object traveling at a constant speed in a circle of radius R, with a time period T. Communications satellites orbit the Earth, receiving signals from the ground and retransmitting them to another satellite or back to Earth. This allows phones, computers, and other electronic devices to communicate between any two points in the world. Earth-based transmitters have to track where the nearest satellite is located at any moment in order to send it a signal. A geosynchronous orbit, one with a period of exactly T = 24 hours, makes this tracking easy. (To stay exactly over a single place on the Earth, orbit must be over the equator too.) A satellite orbiting the Earth is like a planet orbiting the Sun. As noted in Table 2.1, Kepler's third law predicts that a certain radius (R) gives us a certain period. It turns out that for a geosynchronous orbit of the Earth, R = 35,800 km (about six times the radius of the Earth itself).

Equations 5.1 and 5.2 tell us how fast the satellite is moving and at what rate it is accelerating. Using them, we get $v = 2\pi R/T =$ 9369 km/hr, and $a = 2\pi v/T = 2453$ km/hr^2. This is fast; commercial airliners have a maximum speed of around 850 km/hr, which is less than 1/10 as fast. Is it a large acceleration? Not really, in the sense that it is much less than the acceleration of a ball falling to Earth from your hand, which would be $a = 9.8$ m/s^2 = 12,700 km/hr^2. In the next section, we talk about motion near the Earth, for which objects accelerate at this rate, symbolized as g, where $g = 9.8$ m/s^2. The force of gravity from the Earth is making both the ball and the satellite accelerate. The ball is closer to the planet than the satellite, and this means the Earth can make the ball accelerate more. Later in this book, when we talk about the forces that create accelerations, we'll return to this idea.

PARABOLAS IN TIME AND SPACE

In an airport or another public space, you might see the kind of fountain with "dancing water," in which streams of water are controlled by valves that open and close in a preprogrammed way

(Figure 5.2). The water follows the graceful arc of a parabola. There is nothing special in the fountain mechanism that makes the water follow this curve. A parabola is the natural shape that any object will pursue as it travels under the influence of a uniform acceleration, in this case, a vertical acceleration that comes from the Earth's gravity. This point really hits home if you watch the fountain long enough to see one of the valves alternately open and close for brief periods of time. Rather than a continuous stream of water, a short "tube" of water exits the nozzle. It follows the same arc that the continuous stream did with a motion reminiscent of an acrobat jumping through an invisible hoop (Figure 5.3).

Figure 5.2 *The dancing water fountain located at the Detroit Metropolitan Wayne County Airport.*

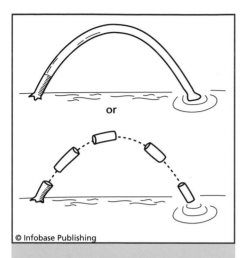

Figure 5.3 *A stream of water, whether uninterrupted, or interrupted into short bursts, follows a parabolic trajectory.*

The interdependence of horizontal, $x(t)$, and vertical, $y(t)$, positions determines the **trajectory**, $y(x)$. Figure 5.3 shows a trajectory of water droplets. We will use the idea of velocity and acceleration vectors in order to understand a trajectory. Let's break a single water droplet's velocity vector into components. Consider the droplet's velocity vector as the sum of horizontal and vertical velocity vectors as in Figure 5.4a. At a time t, let's call the sizes of the horizontal and vertical velocities $v_x(t)$ and $v_y(t)$.

We will use the fundamental equation $\delta v = a\delta t$. (In fact, because a is a constant, there is no difference between average and instantaneous acceleration, and we are allowed to say $\Delta v = a\Delta t$ for any size time interval, Δt.) Because the acceleration vector, a, points downward, $v_y(t)$ will change. It grows in a downward sense, just like the velocity of the cliff diver discussed in Chapter 3. But $v_x(t)$ will stay constant in time. Figure 5.4b shows this in a pictorial way. The path that is tangent to this series of velocity vectors is $y(x)$. (This all assumes that we disregard air resistance, which in reality will slow the water droplets a bit in both the horizontal and vertical directions.)

There is another way to find the shape of the trajectory of projectiles, such as a drop of water or a ball, with a calculation that Olivia from Chapter 3 might do. In Chapter 3, we saw that an object accelerating at a constant rate has a height $y(t)$ whose *time* dependence is described with a parabola:

$$y(t) = y_0 + v_{y0}t - 1/2 \, gt^2 \qquad (5.3)$$

The Shortest Distance Between Two Points

Let g = 0 in Equation 5.5, and you see that $y(x) = (v_{y0}/v_{x0})$ x. This is a straight line (with slope equal to v_{y0}/v_{x0}). A "free particle" moves in a straight line. But why does that happen? A straight line is the shortest distance between two points. What difference does that make? In the 17th century, physicists tried to uncover the grand principle that would explain why straight lines are special to nature. The grand principle would also explain why other trajectories, like the parabolic trajectory of a ball or the elliptical trajectory of a planet, are special in those other situations.

The idea that a free particle takes the quickest path between its starting and ending points is called the "principle of least time." Ancient Greek and Arabic scientists stated this principle for paths of rays of light. Pierre de Fermat is the 17th century European figure known for proposing it. The quickest path is the shortest path, hence a straight line. Fermat's principle was made more powerful a century later by physicists who said that not time, but a quantity called "action" was minimized by a thrifty nature. The "principle of least action" worked for light, a free particle, a falling ball, an orbiting planet, and everything else. Yet in the 20th century, Albert Einstein brought us back to the geometrical idea of shortest path. He showed how a parabola, ellipse, etc...*was* the shortest path (a "geodesic") between two points, when space and time were curved in the presence of gravity.

In Equation 5.3, the vertical position at time zero is y_0, and vertical component of the velocity vector is v_{y0}. Say that water emerges from a hose that we use to water a new tree, as in Figure 5.5. For simplicity, say that the mouth of the hose defines the starting positions as $x_0 = 0$ and $y_0 = 0$. The horizontal coordinate undergoes uniform motion. That is,

$$x(t) = v_{x0}t \tag{5.4}$$

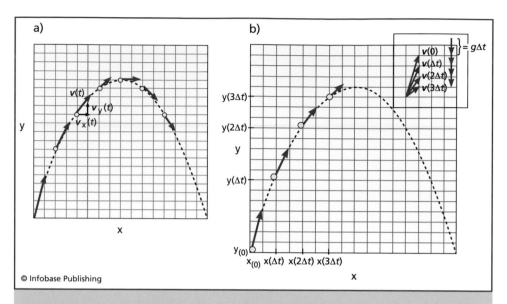

Figure 5.4 *(a) The velocity vector of a drop of water at various moments during its flight. At any time (t) the vector (v) can be broken up into a horizontal vector of size $v_x(t)$ and a vertical vector of size $v_y(t)$. (b) The velocity vector of a drop of water at various moments, separated by time Δt. These vectors are redrawn in the box on the upper right side of the graph, where you can see that in each time interval, Δt, the vertical component of the velocity, v_y, has been reduced by a factor gΔt, and the horizontal component, v_x, remains the same.*

where the horizontal part of the velocity vector is constant, equal to its initial value v_{xo}. Now rearrange Equation 5.4 by dividing by v_{xo}. In other words, time is related to horizontal position as:

$$t = x/v_{xo}$$

Now substituting this into Equation 5.3 for $y(t)$, we find the parabolic trajectory we expect:

$$y(x) = (v_{yo}/v_{xo})\, x - (g/v_{xo}^2)\, x^2 \qquad (5.5)$$

The parabolic trajectory of an arc of water, or of any **projectile**, owes its shape to the fact that it is accelerating vertically and moving at constant speed horizontally. The parabola in Equation 5.5 arches downward, since a negative number, $-(g/v_{xo}^2)$, multiplies the x^2 term.

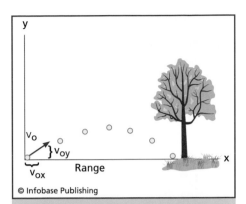

© Infobase Publishing

Figure 5.5 *The circle at the bottom left represents a garden hose. The range of the stream of water is the horizontal distance that it travels. Range depends on both initial speed (v_o) and angle. The range gives the horizontal distance from the nozzle of the hose to the base of tree at the same height as the nozzle.*

We often care about a projectile that rises and falls back to its original height, say, $y = 0$. In other words, we care about the two roots of the function $y(x)$, the two x values such that $y(x) = 0$. The distance between these two roots is the distance that the water drop covers along the ground, also known as the **range** of the water's trajectory. Suppose you want to water a young tree where the base of the tree is at the same height as the hose nozzle, as in Figure 5.5. How far would you place the nozzle from the tree in order to do the job? Suppose that the water leaves the hose with vertical speed $v_{yo} = 5.0$ m/sec and horizontal speed $v_{xo} = 3.0$ m/sec. Substituting the numbers into Equation 5.5, we get

$$y(x) = (5/3)x - (9.8/9)x^2 \text{ with } x \text{ and } y \text{ in meters, so}$$

$$y(x) = 1.67x - 1.09x^2$$

This function $y(x)$ has two roots: $x = 0$ and $x = 1.53$ m. So 1.53 m is the range of the water's trajectory. It is the distance from the base of the tree at which you place the nozzle.

OTHER ACCELERATED MOTIONS: FLIGHT TRAINING

Writing the acceleration in multiples of $g = 9.8$ m/sec², the acceleration of an object falling freely toward the ground, is common when dealing with accelerations with human consequences. For example, the safety standard for trained pilots is that they do not exceed about 7 g's. Among other problems, high acceleration upward means that oxygenated blood has trouble fighting its way from your heart to your brain. (Military pilots wearing special g-suits can experience greater accelerations for short periods of time as part of their training.) Here we explore two maneuvers involving acceleration of pilots and passengers.

A "touch and go" is a training maneuver. The pilot must prepare to land and touch the wheels of the plane down on the runway. The plane must decelerate to a speed that is less than the speed necessary to keep it airborne. Then the pilot accelerates, lifts off, and gains altitude again. This is the type of training one needs in order to be prepared for an emergency "go-around," where a hazardous condition is detected on the runway.

Suppose a plane has touched down on the runway and is moving horizontally at a speed of 35 m/s (about 78 miles/hour). A short time of $\Delta t = 1$ second later, it has accelerated to a speed of 40 m/s (about 90 miles/hour) and has lifted off so that it is

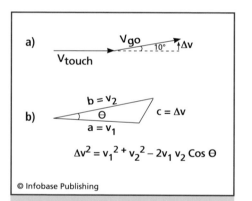

© Infobase Publishing

Figure 5.6 *(a) During $\Delta t = 1$ sec of a touch-and-go maneuver, a plane rises by an angle of 10° from the runway, while its speed changes from 35 to 40 m/sec. (b) The law of cosines can be used to find the acceleration, $\Delta v/\Delta t$, of the plane. The lengths of the legs a, b, and c of the triangle represent the speeds v_1, v_2, and Δv.*

ascending at an angle of 10° above the horizontal (Figure 5.6a). What is the average acceleration of the plane?

We can draw the velocity vectors using a protractor to construct the 10° angle. In this way, we find Δv, which will form the third side of a triangle. How to find the length of Δv? One way is just with a ruler. If the other two legs have length 35 and 40, Δv seems to be a little more than 8 m/s long. Alternatively, we can use algebra to find Δv, thanks to a trigonometric rule called the law of cosines, which says that

$$c^2 = a^2 + b^2 - 2\,ab\,\cos\theta \qquad\qquad (5.6)$$

Using this rule with v_1, v_2 and Δv playing the role of a, b and c, and with $\theta = 10°$, we find that $\Delta v = 8.2$ m/s. So we've found the size of the average acceleration to be

$$a = \Delta v/\Delta t = 8.2 \text{ m/s}/1.0 \text{ s} = 8.2 \text{ m/s}^2 = 0.84\ g$$

A plane has three different axes through its center about which it can rotate. Rotations about these three axes are given the names pitch, yaw, and roll. When a plane pitches, its nose moves up or down. Yaw involves the nose moving horizontally, left or right. Rolling involves the wings dipping. Suppose that two acrobatic flyers want to perform a roll in an air show. The plane will fly level, but roll about the axis through the nose of the plane, so that everything in the plane undergoes uniform circular motion. Figure 5.7 shows the pilot with head 1 meter above the nose of the plane. The acceleration of the pilot's head turns out to be $a = 19.6$ m/s^2, or 2 g. The second acrobat is going to thrill the crowd by spending the flight strapped to the end of the wing, 4 m away from the nose of the plane. Is this person in danger from accelerating at a rate that is unsafe (greater than, say, 7 g)?

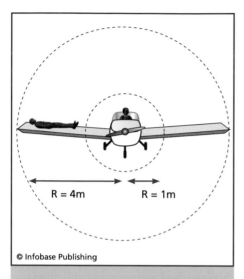

Figure 5.7 *Two acrobatic flyers, hoping to do a roll to entertain spectators. The acceleration of one of them (or of a single body part, like a head) is proportional to the distance, R, from the center of rotation.*

Like the bugs at the beginning of the chapter, the acceleration of an object will be proportional to its distance, R, from the center of rotation; that is, in Equation 5.2:

$$a \propto R$$

Though the pilot is safe because his head accelerates at 2 g, the person on the wing will accelerate with

$$a = 2\,g\,(4\ m/1\ m) = 8\,g$$

This trick should be rethought!

CONCLUSION: ROLLER COASTERS AND G-FORCES

Dr. Kelp explains that traditional roller coasters use power only to raise the chain of cars to the top of the first big drop. After that, they coast—hence their name. Lori gets a flash of insight. A roller coaster car accelerates under gravity, something like the drops of water in Figure 5.3. As the car crests a hill, its speed is lowest, like a drop at the top of its arc in Figure 5.4a. As it swoops through a valley, its speed is high, like a drop lower in its arc. Moreover, the valley is a section of curved track. The car accelerates toward the center of the curve, much like the bug on the clock in Figure 5.1a. Lori gets a picture like Figure 5.8 in her mind. She explains to the class that, like in uniform circular motion, acceleration, a, is large when v is large. Also, acceleration points toward the center of the circle, which at that point in the track is upward. So at the bottom of the valley, the vectors *g* and *−a* are parallel to each other, giving a strong g-force on the car and its riders, of size *g* + *a*.

The class went on to argue about which car and what coaster would give the most exciting ride. Some people enjoy rocketing forward in the last car that is whipped over the top of a hill by all the cars ahead that are plummeting downward. Others love the terrifying "hang time" at the top when, because *a* = *g* there, and in this situation of a zero g-force, they would feel weightless. Still others like the loops, where g-forces create a kind of artificial gravity that pins riders to the seat. Lori and her friends discovered that the exciting parts of the rides were all tied to the phenomenon of acceleration.

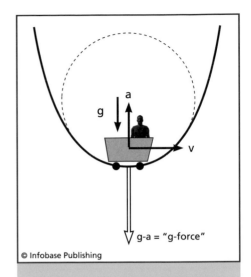

© Infobase Publishing

Figure 5.8 *The acceleration (a) and g vectors. Because the car's acceleration is high and directed opposite to that of gravity, the riders experienced a large g-force.*

CHAPTER 6

Forces: What They Are and What They Do

ASHOK AND HIS FRIENDS ARE INTO SCIENCE FICTION BOOKS and films. They like it when the engineering or science parts of these films are done right. They also enjoy ridiculing a film when it makes an obvious mistake. In one recent film, the heroes were about to be sent to their deaths by being forced out of the airlock of an enemy spaceship. Warning lights were flashing, and there was noise and steam as the chamber began to depressurize. Suddenly a trapdoor opened and the heroes dropped into the void of space, where they floated for a few seconds until they were rescued in a very improbable way!

Afterward, back at Ashok's house, the friends were dissecting the scene. They got into a debate about exactly what would happen if you were just above a trapdoor that suddenly opened into empty space. Would you fall out or just float near the door? What would it feel like outside? Could you somehow get yourself turned around and back to the door to climb into the ship again?

Ashok wondered what was so dangerous about being in empty space without a suit. Yeah, people need to breathe. But if you could hold your breath until someone rescued you, would you be okay? He had read somewhere that your lungs would explode. He knew that ideas from physics about gravity and air pressure would help him understand motion and survival in outer space.

In this chapter, we will be able to understand situations like the one in Ashok's film by talking about the concept of force. We'll talk about what kinds of forces exist in the universe, and what kinds of motions are possible in the absence of force.

THE FORCES OF NATURE

In a dictionary, you may encounter several definitions of force before you get to a scientific one, like the following:

> **4 a :** *an agency or influence that if applied to a free body results chiefly in an acceleration of the body and sometimes in elastic deformation and other effects* **b :** *any of the natural influences (as electromagnetism, gravity, the strong force, and the weak force) that exist especially between particles and determine the structure of the universe*[13]

This definition still doesn't tell what force *is*; it tells what it *does* to something called a *free body*. Force is evidently so fundamental that it resists being defined. For our convenience in studying force and motion, we divide forces up into **contact forces**, where the interacting objects touch, and **action-at-a-distance forces**, where they do not. There is nothing fundamental about these two categories; they simply help us organize our thoughts to solve real-world force/motion problems. In fact, if we look deep into the small-scale structure of matter, when the concept of touching loses its meaning, we realize that all contact forces are the result of an action-at-a-distance force: electromagnetism. Another action-at-a-distance force is gravity, which keeps the Earth from disintegrating, keeps us stuck to its surface, and

TABLE 6.1   Contact Forces

NAME	SYMBOL	IN A NUTSHELL . . .	SOME THINGS IT DOES . . .
normal force	F_N	The atoms of a solid are bonded together into a pattern. They resist an outside object that tries to invade their surface and break the pattern. Unless it is so stressed that it bends or breaks, a solid surface exerts just the right amount of force, the normal force, directed perpendicular to itself, to keep two solid objects apart.	Allows you to lean against a wall, slide down a slide, or stand on the floor without gravity pulling you right through the surface.
frictional force	F_f	When two surfaces are in close contact, the molecules of each pull and push laterally against each other. Frictional force is directed parallel to the two surfaces, to inhibit or even prevent them sliding across each other. In general, the rougher the surface(s) on a molecular level, and the more closely the surfaces are pressed together, the greater the frictional force.	Allows bike and car brakes to work; enables you to walk and run. (Without friction, your feet would slip smoothly backward and you would forever run in place.)
fluid resistance	D	Fluid resistance acts to oppose motion through air, water, etc. For slow and/or small objects fluid resistance is proportional to speed. For fast and/or large objects, fluid resistance is proportional to speed squared. Fluid resistance comes mostly from the difference in pressure between the fluid in front of (higher pressure) and behind (lower pressure) the object. Since force = pressure x area, the larger the object's cross-sectional area, the larger the fluid resistance force.	Makes swimming good exercise; requires an opposite force, "thrust," in order for planes to have a forward motion; makes parachutes work.

NAME	SYMBOL	IN A NUTSHELL . . .	SOME THINGS IT DOES . . .
tension	T	The force transmitted by a rope when you exert a force on one (or both) end(s).	Allows you to use ropes and pulleys; keeps suspension bridges up.
spring force	F_s	All solid objects have some springiness; a force that pushes back when you push and pulls back when you pull. Real springs (coiled-up objects usually made of metal) magnify the effect. A spring force is an idealization; it always acts in the direction opposite to motion, and has a strength that, for small deviations from some neutral position, is proportional to that deviation.	Makes car shock absorbers work; allows people to bungee jump; allows old fashioned watches to keep time; allows buildings and bridges to constantly adjust to the stresses of wind and usage.
buoyant force	F_B	An object submerged partially (or totally) in water, air, etc., will feel a buoyant force proportional to the weight of fluid that would have occupied the submerged part (or whole).	Allows boats to float (even ones with concrete in their hulls); allows fish to swim easily; makes life jackets work. (They weigh little, but take up space of water that weighs much more.)

keeps the Earth revolving around the Sun. As much as Newton understood about gravity, it troubled him throughout his life that he could never identify a concrete thing that mediated this action-at-a-distance.

Table 6.1 outlines the contact forces that often affect motion. Table 6.2 lists the fundamental action-at-a-distance forces of

TABLE 6.2 The Four Fundamental Action-at-a-Distance Forces of Nature*			
FORCE	PARTICLE THAT CARRIES IT	SOME PARTICLES THAT FEEL IT	SOME THINGS IT IS RESPONSIBLE FOR
electro-magnetic	Virtual photon	protons**, electrons, . . . every particle with an electric charge as well as some without, like neutrons	lightning, refrigerator magnets, holding molecules together, holding solids together, contact forces
weak	W and Z boson	neutrons**, protons**, electrons, neutrinos	allows particles like neutrinos or quarks to change into different members of their species; produces the kind of radioactivity called "beta decay"
strong	Gluon	gluons***, quarks	holding protons together, holding the atomic nucleus together
gravitation	Graviton****	every particle in the universe	holding planets together, holding stars together, holding galaxies together, the reason you shouldn't jump off tall buildings

* Physicists who work with high energies have a different way of counting forces and will count only three. This is because at high enough energies, it is believed that the fundamental carriers of two of the forces reveal that they are actually the same particle.

** Protons and neutrons are not fundamental particles; they are made of quarks.

*** Gluons are weird. They not only produce the strong force, they also feel the strong force. This is not true of the other three force-producing particles.

**** Some physicists still wonder if gravity is a force like the others, which are produced by the exchange of special particles.

nature. Each of these is considered to be "carried" across empty space by a special fundamental particle. The term *fundamental* just means that no experiment has yet revealed any substructure inside of it. Putting it another way, if any substructure were discovered, we would wonder what force-carrier holds it together. For example, in 1935 the physicist Hideki Yukawa predicted that a new force-carrier, the pion, holds the protons and neutrons together in a nucleus. This strong force counters electrical forces that try to break it apart. Decades later, it was found that the pion was made up of two smaller particles known as quarks. Protons and neutrons are also made of quarks, held together by the strong force. But what carries it? For the last few decades, we have believed that the carrier of the strong force is a fundamental particle known as a gluon.[14]

WEIGHT AND FORCE

"I can't close my suitcase!" complained Ashok's little brother. He was sitting on the top of the bulging case filled with clothes and toys, but his small weight was not enough to make it close sufficiently so he could snap the locks shut. "Will you help me, Ashok?" His big brother took his place sitting on the lid, and it closed. A person's **weight** is the force with which the planet's gravity is pulling down on him or her. The equation for weight is:

$$W = F_{grav}$$

where W symbolizes weight and F_{grav} is the gravitational force. When one of the brothers sits on the lid of the suitcase, this gravitational force is transmitted through the lid and it results in a downward force, W, on the case.

Why is Ashok able to transmit a greater force than his little brother, and how can he exert this force not by using his muscles, but by just sitting down? It turns out that gravitational force on a person or object is proportional to their **mass**, or their physical bulk. Ashok has a greater mass than his little brother, and so he experiences a greater gravitational force—he weighs more. He is thus able to transmit more force in the form of his weight to the suitcase lid. For Ashok or any object of mass M at a planet's surface:

$$W = F_{grav} = Mg \tag{6.1}$$

The constant g is the acceleration due to gravity, which for Earth is the familiar value, $g = 9.8$ m/s². A synonym for g is the **gravitational field**. By dimensional analysis, Equation 6.1 tells us that the units of force in the SI system, Newtons (abbreviated as N), are the same as the units of (mass)(acceleration). In other words:

$$1 \text{ N} = 1 \text{ kg m/s}^2$$

You are probably familiar with people describing their weight in units of pounds (lbs), a unit of force. You can convert your weight in lbs to a weight in the SI unit, Newtons, using the following equation:

$$1 \text{ N} = 0.22 \text{ lb}$$

In England, however, people describe not their weight but their mass, and use the unit of kilograms.

In Table 3.1 you saw the value of g on various planets. Why do they have different gravitational fields? The value g has to do with a few basic properties of the planet that is producing it. One property is its mass (M_p) and in fact

$$g \propto M_p \tag{6.2}$$

Compare a world made entirely of ice (with a mass density of around 0.9 g/cm³) with our world (with an average mass density of around 5.5 g/cm³). If these worlds had exactly the same size and shape, then

$$g_{iceworld}/g_{Earth} = 0.9 / 5.5 = 0.16$$

By Equation 6.1, you will weigh less than 1/6 of your Earth weight when you visit the ice world.

Gravity is a universal phenomenon. If a body has mass, it feels the gravitational field of other bodies, and it produces a gravitational field of its own. A bowling ball and a planet both produce gravitational fields, but the ball simply has too little mass, M_p, (see Equation 6.2) to produce a sizeable g. A mountain is large enough that there is a scientifically detectable increase in the value of g near it. One way of finding mineral deposits in the Earth, which are denser and heavier than surrounding rock, or mapping interesting geological features below the ocean, is to survey a region using a gravitometer, a sensitive device to measure the local value of g.[15]

When you are right next to an object with mass M_p (e.g., you are at the surface of a planet), g will be larger if the object is smaller. In other words, if you are able to get closer to that mass, it will pull on you more strongly. For a spherical body, there is a very simple rule: g is inversely proportional to the square of its radius, R. In other words, a spherical body of mass M_p produces a field:

$$g \propto M_p/R^2 \tag{6.3}$$

If the Earth were made of the same stuff it is now, but compressed so it was half as large (in terms of its radius), we would all weigh four times as much. The extreme limit of mass being compressed happens at the surface of a black hole, an ancient star whose mass has collapsed into an unimaginably small sphere and attracts objects so strongly that light itself is bound into orbit around it.

NATURAL MOTION

The Greek philosopher Aristotle distinguished between natural and violent motion.[16] Motions that were natural were the result of objects choosing how they wanted to move. Fire's natural motion was upward, and a star's natural motion was in circles (as one would infer if one were watching the stars "move" through the night sky from our spinning Earth). On the other hand, violent motions were ones that happened when some agent was forcing the object to undertake them.

This is not such a bad theory for 2,300 years ago. There are indeed motions that are allowed when all force is absent, and different motions that can only occur when an object feels a force. However, it took many more years for people to arrive at the right idea of what was natural (unforced) and what was violent (forced) motion. For example, the kind of motion in which an object circles around a point outside itself is not natural. People in the early medieval era in Europe recognized this. The church-approved view was that the stars, planets, sun, and moon were tugged around in circles by angels.[17]

In Chapter 3, we used the term *uniform motion* to describe motion in a straight line at a constant speed. Now we can tie this with the Aristotelian concept of natural motion by realizing that natural motion is uniform motion. The natural motion for the heroes in Ashok's film is constant velocity in a straight line. If they find themselves drifting away from the ship without external intervention, they are seemingly doomed to remain in that state of motion.

NEWTON'S FIRST LAW

The real world is full of complicated motions and situations. In trying to make predictions that are universally true, physicists usually begin by simplifying the situation. They add the complications in after they understand the basic idea. For example, let us try to write Newton's first law of motion, that uniform motion is unforced motion. We won't capture the true picture on the first try, so we'll try to write it in a series of drafts, simplifying as we go on.

> **Newton's first law** (*First draft*): If there is no force on an object, it does not accelerate.

Let's try out this draft on an "object" that consists of a person attached to a snowboard. (When you snowboard, you are tightly laced into your boots, which are tightly latched to your board.) This is the free body noted in the definition of force at the beginning of the chapter. Picture the snowboarder gliding across a smooth patch of icy snow. If his weight stays even, if he is tucked down low so that the dragging force of the wind is negligible, he continues along in a straight line at a constant speed for a long time.

But what if his nose itches? He can scratch it, but then isn't his hand accelerating? There is still no force. Or is there? Doesn't it take force for him to raise his arm and wiggle his fingers? Our object has moving parts, and we want to simplify and just follow its center. There are many ways you might define the center of the snowboarder + board, but the one that nature singles out to undergo uniform motion in the absence of force is called the **center-of-mass.** The center-of-mass is a mathematical point, situated at the geometrical average of all the mass. We can mentally break up any object into many small chunks: a tiny amount of mass, m_1 at position r_1, m_2 at position r_2, and so on. The center-of-mass is located at R, with

$$R = \frac{1}{M} \sum_i m_i r_i \qquad (6.4)$$

where M is the total amount of mass in the object:

$$M = \sum_i m_i$$

Figure 6.1 depicts the position of the center-of-mass, which physicists usually mark with this symbol, $\otimes$, for a collection of objects. You can raise your center-of-mass by putting on a heavy helmet. You can lower it by putting on heavy boots. Automotive designers, hoping to keep cars handling well and prevent them from rolling during accidents, will usually try to distribute their mass to

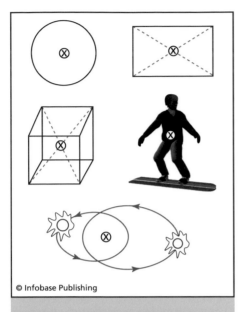

© Infobase Publishing

Figure 6.1 *Centers-of-mass, indicated with the symbol ⊗, of a disk, rectangle, cube, snowboarder, and binary star system with two stars in orbit around each other (in fact, they are in orbit around the fixed point in space that coincides with their center-of-mass).*

keep the center-of-mass as low as possible.

The object we are talking about doesn't have to consist of connected objects. Newton's laws of motion will be just as good at describing a galaxy of disconnected stars, planets, gas, and dust as they are at describing a snowboarder. The center-of-mass does not have to fall on any solid object, as the binary star system in Figure 6.1 shows. The center-of-mass of the Earth + Moon object is a point within the Earth, but the center-of-mass of the Sun + Jupiter object is in empty space, 46,000 km above the surface of the Sun.

TALKING ABOUT PHYSICS: POINT MASSES

Sometimes we ignore the size of objects completely and just treat them as if they were a **point mass**, in other words, a single point at which all the matter in the object is imagined to be concentrated. If an object is very small, or is viewed from very far away, we feel justified in treating it as having essentially no extent. But we often stretch reality and treat other bodies like point masses, when there is justification for believing that only their mass and location affect the property we are measuring. For example, the gravitational force at a distance r from a true point mass is proportional to $1/r^2$. However, as was demonstrated mathematically by C. F. Gauss, a perfectly spherical distribution of mass creates the same gravitational field as a true point mass located at the center of the sphere. Emboldened by nice simplifications like this, physicists feel comfortable approximating many types of objects as point masses.

NEWTON'S FIRST LAW REVISED

With these concepts in mind, let's revise Newton's first law.

> **Newton's first law** (*Second draft*): If there is no force on an object, its center-of-mass doesn't accelerate.

This second draft is better, but it is still not as helpful as it might be. We have not cleared up what it means for a force to act on an extended object. We need better definitions of forces.

A force can be external or internal to an object. Internal forces are ones that act between its parts; external forces come from the outside. Obviously, whether a force is internal or external to a thing depends on how you define the object. If the Earth is an object, the Sun's gravity is external to it. On the other hand, if you want to view our whole solar system as an object, gravity between the sun and the planets is an internal force that holds the solar system together. Internal forces are inevitable if any real object is to keep its integrity. The snowboarder's ligaments keep his bones and muscles together. On a microscopic level, his cells cling to each other with internal forces, and on a submicroscopic level, so do his atoms. When the snowboarder uses his arm muscles to wiggle his fingers, internal forces are acting. Wind resistance, on the other hand, is an external force that will slow him down. If the terrain starts to slope downhill, the external force of gravity will speed him up.

Internal forces cannot budge the center-of-mass. It will be easier to appreciate this fact when we introduce Newton's third law in Chapter 7. For now we will treat it as a given and create another draft of the law.

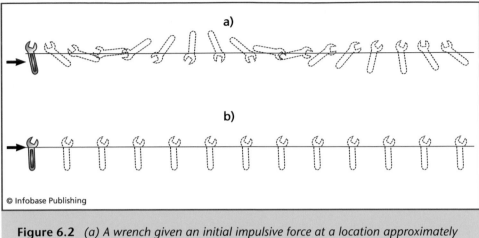

Figure 6.2 *(a) A wrench given an initial impulsive force at a location approximately indicated by the arrow, moves in a complicated manner, yet its center-of-mass (the part of the wrench intersected by the yellow line) is in a uniform state of motion. (b) The same wrench is given an initial impulsive force right at its center-of-mass, so that it moves uniformly but does not spin.*

> **Newton's first law** (*Third draft*): If there is no external force on an object, its center-of-mass doesn't accelerate.

Does motion depend on where the force acts on an object that is clearly not a point mass? Yes and no.[18] In Figure 6.2a, someone has struck a wrench to send it spinning across a smooth, slippery tabletop. The wrench does something complicated, but its center of mass moves very simply, executing uniform motion. In Figure 6.2b, we see the result of striking the wrench at the center of mass itself. Now the entire wrench executes uniform motion. The bottom line is that the detailed motion of the entire object depends on where the force is applied. But it is immaterial to the motion of its center-of-mass, which is the subject of Newton's first law.

Here is one final refinement to the idea of force. Take the ends of a pen in both of your hands, and pull equally hard, left

and right. The pen is going no-
where; it is in a state of uniform
motion. But aren't you exerting
an external force on it? In fact,
there are *two* distinct external
forces acting on it coming from
your hands. Forces are vectors,
and when more than one force
acts on a body, we add them up
according to the rules of vector addition.

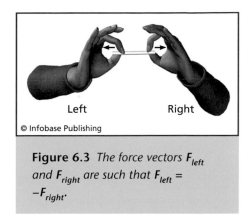

Left   Right

© Infobase Publishing

Figure 6.3 *The force vectors F_{left} and F_{right} are such that $F_{left} = -F_{right}$.*

The sum of all forces act-
ing on an object is called the **net
force**. If you exert equal and opposite forces with each hand, as in
Figure 6.3, there is no net force on the pen. This brings us to the
final draft of Newton's first law. The final draft is not only true
(like the second and third drafts), but is maximally useful.

> **Newton's first law** (*Final draft!*): If there is no net external
> force on an object, its center-of-mass doesn't accelerate.

When we analyze a problem about the motion of an object, we
look for the many sources of external force on it and add them up.
When an object has no external forces acting on it at all, physicists
call it an isolated system. Of course, in an isolated system Newton's first law applies, but it may apply as well to a non-isolated
system when the net external force on it is zero.

FORCE-BODY DIAGRAMS

As mentioned previously, force is a vector quantity. When we
draw an object and all the sources of force exerted on it, for the
purpose of summing them to determine the net force vector, we
are drawing what is called a **force-body diagram**.

Figure 6.4 *On the left a person is lying in bed. On the right is a force-body diagram depicting the situation.*

Say you are lying in bed, not accelerating. There are forces on you—gravity is pulling on your body with F_g, a force vector of size Mg and direction downward. But the bed is exerting a normal force, F_N (see Table 6.1), that is exactly equal and opposite to that of gravity. In the force-body diagram in Figure 6.4, the body (you) is represented as a simple shape, like a box, so that the force vectors extend from it in the correct directions. The force vector arrows are drawn to be the same size, indicating that the two magnitudes are the same, though their directions are opposite.

Our logic about the normal force is circular—we admit it. When you see something resting comfortably on a surface, (like you on the bed) you assume that F_N is as strong as it needs to be to keep it there. F_N is always directed perpendicular (or normal, hence the name) to the surface and will be just strong enough to keep an object from going through it. In this case, F_N has a strength that is equal to the force of gravity, F_g. In symbols:

$$F_g + F_N = 0; \; F_g = -F_N \qquad (6.5)$$

We have faith that Equation 6.4 is right precisely because we see Newton's first law in action. There no net acceleration of your center-of-mass, hence no net force on you.

Let's look at force-body diagrams for the snowboarder in a few situations: on flat ground, with the wind blowing, and on a downslope. On the flat ground, there are external forces on the snowboarder, even on flat ground with no wind, but they are the same forces that would act on the person lying in bed: F_g pointing down and F_N pointing up (Figure 6.5a).

With air resistance, there is a dragging force from the air that the boarder moves through. The conventional notation for drag is **D** (see Sidebar 6.1). So Figure 6.5b is not a situation where Newton's first law applies. The net force is horizontal in direction and has magnitude D.

The forces for a snowboarder on a downhill slope are diagrammed in Figure 6.5c. On the downsloping surface, the normal force F_N points straight up from the surface, so it is not a situation where it balances gravity to produce a zero net force:

$$F_N + F_g = F_{net} \neq 0$$

The net force, F_{net}, is found by taking a vector sum, which we can do either geometrically, by tip-to-tail adding, or by breaking the forces into horizontal and vertical components, as in Figure 6.5d, where the thick purple arrow is F_{net}. Notice that the direction of the net force is along the surface. This must be true if we make the correct choice and let F_N cancel the component of the gravitational force that points into the surface.

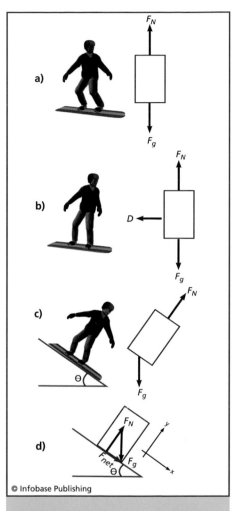

© Infobase Publishing

Figure 6.5 *Various force-body diagrams for different snowboarding conditions. (a) Boarder glides along level ground. (b) Boarder slows down while feeling a drag force from the wind. (c) Boarder navigates a downslope. (d) Constructing the net force vector F_{net} (thick purple arrow) by adding F_N and F_g tip-to-tail.*

Suppose we say that the slope has angle θ and we would like to know the net force. Then:

$$F_{net,y} = F_N - F_g \cos\theta = F_N - Mg \cos\theta = 0 \qquad (6.6a)$$

$$F_{net,x} = F_g \sin\theta = Mg \sin\theta \qquad (6.6b)$$

Equation 6.5a says that the normal force is "just as strong as it needs to be" to keep the motion along the slope. In this case, it "needs to be" $F_N = Mg \cos\theta$. The unbalanced component of the force, in the horizontal direction along the slope, is the net force.

$$F_{net} = Mg \sin\theta \text{ in the } x \text{ direction, along the slope}$$

If $\theta = 0$, then $\sin\theta = 0$ so $F_{net} = 0$. We are back to the situation on flat ground, where there is no net force and no acceleration. The more severe the slope, the larger is $\sin\theta$, and the greater is the net force. The limiting case of the hill being a vertical cliff would have $\theta = 90°$, thus $\sin\theta = 1$. The net force downward would be equal to the full force of gravity.

AIR PRESSURE

The **pressure** on a surface is the component of force directed straight toward (that is, normal to) the surface, divided by the area of surface. For example, when Ashok, whose weight is W, sits on a rigid suitcase lid of area A, the pressure he exerts on the lid is P, where:

$$P = F_{grav}/A = W/A$$

The smaller the lid, the larger the pressure (P) his weight is able to exert.

In the SI system, the units of pressure are N/m^2. Another name for N/m^2 is Pascal (Pa). But there is another unit of pressure, atmospheres (atm). The air in our atmosphere exerts pressure on every surface. Why? Bounce a ball off the palm of your hand—the ball delivers a force that we call "impulsive" (it acts briefly and then is over). Air molecules, like the ball, are moving at about 300 m/sec, though in a random and unorganized way. They will impart an impulsive force, hence a pressure to a surface. Consider, for example, a wall of an empty milk carton. The wall has area A and feels a force from the air both inside and out. It is unaccelerated, so by Newton's first law, the net force on it must be zero. That is $F_{inside} = -F_{outside}$. Thus, the pressures inside and outside have an equal size $P = F_{inside}/A = F_{outside}/A$.

Pressure is the force, per unit area, on either side of any surface you put in the Earth's atmosphere. A good rough estimate is that at sea level the pressure of the atmosphere is around 10 N/cm^2. (The number changes depending on temperature, air humidity, and so on.) What determines its size? Our atmosphere is held to our planet with the force of gravity. The atmospheric pressure at any place is the weight, per unit area, of all the air that exists above it. To find pressure, P_{atm}, we take the weight (W_{air}) of a column of area A, and then divide it by A:

$$P_{atm} = W_{air}/A$$

In other words, the atmosphere contained in a long vertical cylinder of cross section $A = 1$ cm^2 has a weight of approximately 10 N. (The accepted definition of the official unit of pressure known as an atm of pressure is actually 1 atm = 10.12 N/cm^2.) At a higher point in the atmosphere, for a few reasons including the fact that the column is less high, the pressure is less. On Mount Everest, the pressure is only about 1/3 atm.

A milk carton would implode and crumple if we took the air out of the inside, subjecting it to the unbalanced pressure force from the outside. Like that carton, we have 10N (the weight of 1 kg mass) pressing in on each 1 cm^2 of our skin from all sides. Our bodies do not crumple; we are built to supply the needed internal pressure to balance it. We can even control our internal pressures. Our lungs are situated in a chest cavity, like balloons hung in an airtight container. In order to breathe in or out, we change the pressure in the container slightly. When we raise our internal pressure above P_{atm}, our lungs force the air out and we exhale. We lower the pressure in our chest cavity to inhale. How do we make these pressure changes happen? We do it by changing the size of our chest cavity, thanks to muscles like the diaphragm and the muscles between our ribs. The inverse relationship between the volume of a container (V) and the pressure, P, of the gas is known as Boyle's law:

$$P \propto 1/V$$

WHAT WOULD LIFE BE LIKE IN A WORLD WITHOUT FORCES?

Reading this page, you are feeling gravity pulling you down, normal force pushing you up, and air pressure pressing at you from all sides. As long as you are moving uniformly, you are experiencing no net force. You are always feeling forces, though. Darwinian evolution has prepared us to live on the surface of a planet that is tugging at us with a g-force of 1 g and air pressing on us. From head to toe, the human body has structures that expect these pressure and gravitational forces and the body can sense unusual forces (and possibly even find them exciting, like Lori's class in Chapter 5).

For example, our bones are full of minerals, laid down in a lattice-like network to withstand force. When astronauts spend time far above Earth's surface, where the gravitational force is weak, or when people on Earth become inactive (for example, bedridden for a long illness), the load-bearing bones of the legs, hips, and spine are likely to weaken. Normally, your body has bone-constructor cells that lay down new bone about the rate that old bone is dismantled by bone-destructor cells, but the construction lags behind when you are inactive. Running, bungee jumping, and other ways of applying a large amount of force to the affected bones encourages your bone constructors to boost production in order to keep up.

A glimpse of what life might be like under conditions of a reduced gravitational force comes from sea life near the surface of the ocean. In water, the buoyant force upward from the water can partially or totally cancel gravity. The fragile, "low-gravity" plants and animals on a coral reef in the ocean could never exist on land. Nevertheless, this aquatic life exists in a force-filled world. All sea animals that have a method of locomotion (such as fins, tentacles, or jet propulsion—in the case of the clam, jellyfish, and the sea squirt).[19] They rely on the force exerted on them by the surrounding water in order to get from place to place. The principle of you walking forward thanks to a frictional push from the floor and you swimming forward thanks to a push from the water are not so different.[20] In thinking about the film heroes trying to get back to the ship, the idea of "swimming" to move forward in space crosses Ashok's mind. He quickly rejects it. There is nothing in space to swim against to provide a push.

CONCLUSION: IN SPACE, NO ONE CAN HEAR YOU SCREAM

What would have happened to a hero when the airlock opened and he was released into empty space? First off, it is a good thing that the airlock was depressurized gradually. Otherwise, as Ashok had guessed, any air in the hero's lungs would have exerted an unbalanced force outward. For the same reason that a carton empty of both milk and air will implode in Earth's atmosphere, an air-filled milk carton will explode if it is placed in a vacuum. So the hero's lungs would have suffered "explosive decompression" and would have ruptured.

Astronauts wear suits that supply a positive pressure over their whole body so that various molecules stay in their proper proportions within their tissues, in accord with Newton's first law. In the zero pressure environment of space, gases like water vapor would form and try to make their way out. As they filled the outer tissues of his body, the movie hero would start to swell up—very uncomfortable and unattractive, though not necessarily fatal.[21] However, another of the gases that would try to make its way out would be the oxygen in his bloodstream. Even someone trained to hold his or her breath for many minutes cannot maintain normal brain function for more than 10 to 20 seconds if the blood circulating through the brain is devoid of oxygen. There are a few reported incidents of real people accidentally exposed to near space-like vacuum. One occurred at NASA in 1982. The survivor made a full recovery, despite the fact that his "last conscious memory is the water on his tongue beginning to boil."[22]

Regarding the hero's motion: If there is still air pressure in the airlock when the door opens, he will be drawn out into space. Pressure is no longer equal on all sides of him, but is less on the side facing the airlock. All objects that are not fastened down will feel a net force from this difference in pressure and will be swept into the void. On the other hand, if all of the air is gone from the lock when the door opens, and if there is no artificial gravity keeping him standing upright on the floor of the ship, then he will continue as he had been (floating in the airlock) when the door opens.

Suppose that the hero ends up floating a few meters from the door, outside the ship, as in Figure 6.6. (The ship is moving and he shares its velocity (v). He'd like to reach the door and climb back inside. Ashok's friends argue that, based on Newton's first law, the hero cannot possibly propel himself back to the door.

But Ashok realizes that there is hope. Suppose the hero is carrying some expendable object on his person. It is the not the center-of-mass of the hero, but rather the hero + object that remains in uniform motion. If the hero were carrying, say, a large book in his pocket, he could throw it in a direction opposite to the way he wants to move. Figure 6.6 shows how he and the book would move afterward. The center-of-mass of hero + book remains as before, and as the book moves at a uniform speed, in relative terms moving away from the airlock, the hero moves (even more slowly, in proportion to his greater mass) toward the airlock. Throwing the book harder so that it acquires a greater speed rela-

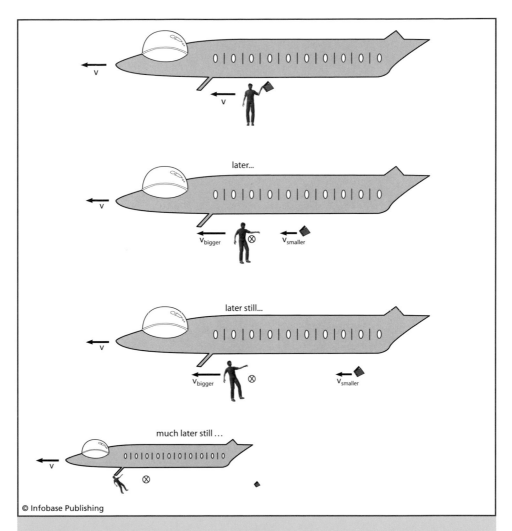

© Infobase Publishing

Figure 6.6 *The hero and the book are, at first, keeping pace with the alien ship, all traveling at speed **v** to the left. The center of mass continues to do so, but by throwing the book to the right, it attains a slightly lower speed **v**$_{smaller}$, and the hero a slightly greater speed **v**$_{bigger}$. The upshot is that the hero begins to catch up with the open hatch. The book, while moving to the left in absolute terms, is moving to the right with respect to the ship and the hero. If the hero is more massive (in this picture, about 5 or 6 times as massive) as the book, the extra speed he picks up is 5 or 6 times smaller than that of the book. This will ensure that the center of mass continues moving as it did before, at speed **v** to the left, in accordance with Newton's first law.*

tive to himself, and/or throwing a heavier book, would get him to the airlock even more quickly.

This idea of throwing some extra mass in one direction to propel a payload in the opposite direction is the idea behind rockets, jet planes, aquatic animals like squids, and so on. The reason that a rocket explosively burns fuel is to get it moving away from the payload at the largest possible speed, just as throwing the book harder will get the hero moving faster.

Rescued by Newton's first law and a book! All of Ashok's friends agreed it would be physically possible. But they all agreed that they still liked the film as it was, with a rescue ship traveling instantaneously across space and time and materializing next to him. A fantastic new physical law was needed to provide a propulsion system for this rescue ship, and the friends proceeded to argue about that late into the night.

CHAPTER 7

Forces and Accelerations

"STOP RIGHT THERE . . . RIGHT NOW!" SCREAMED MOLLY, as a little creature darted past her and toward the road that separated her from the playground ahead. Miraculously, for once, Bai Lee actually listened to Molly. She skidded to a stop, the toes of her green high-top sneakers coming to rest about a centimeter from the curb. Molly grabbed Bai Lee's hand and held it firmly until the approaching bus had lumbered by and the road was clear.

"How many times have I told you to look both ways?"

"I did! That bus was going slow. I'm fast. I can run 5 miles an hour. I could have made it!"

At this point, Molly couldn't resist showing a little of the knowledge she'd picked up in her physics course with Dr. Kelp. "If the bus is going 20 miles an hour, it is going four times as fast as you. So it can travel 4 street widths in the time you can cover only one."

"The bus was more than 4 street widths away!"

"And what if you tripped?"

"What if? The bus was going so slow; it didn't look like it could hurt me if it bumped me."

Molly really liked this summer job, taking care of the smart and spirited Bai Lee. She wanted to explain the physics to this child, that the force on a pedestrian if a vehicle "bumped" her was great enough to kill her, either when she made contact with the vehicle or when she landed on the hard road surface. However, Bai Lee had spotted a friend at the playground and, debate forgotten, raced away. Molly sat down on a vacant swing and thought about how force relates to acceleration.

In this chapter, we see that net forces create accelerations. The size of the acceleration is proportional to the mass of the object and its direction is parallel to the force. We also see that force is a two-way street. If A exerts a force on B, then B exerts an equal and opposite force on A. At every moment during a collision between a person A and a bus B, the mutual forces are exactly the same in strength. Yet the different properties of A and B, especially their different masses, mean that the resulting motions of A and B will be very different.

FORCES CREATE ACCELERATIONS: NEWTON'S SECOND LAW

In Chapter 6, we discussed objects which experienced no net force, so they moved uniformly. But an object feeling unbalanced forces will accelerate. Net force and acceleration are proportional. The constant accelerations that we discussed in Chapter 3 would arise from a constant net force. Even if the force changes in time, this proportionality holds at every moment and is called Newton's second law:

$$F_{net} = Ma \qquad (7.1)$$

In Equation 7.1, M refers to the mass of the object, and a is the acceleration of its center-of-mass. As a vector equation, it says that the directions of F_{net} and a are parallel; and their sizes obey $F_{net} = Ma$. Turning this around, we realize that the size of acceleration is *inversely* proportional to the mass (M) of the object feeling the force:

$$a = F_{net}/M \qquad (7.2)$$

For example, Molly has brought 3 balls to the playground to pitch to Bai Lee. The balls are roughly the same size, but Ball 1 is a Wiffle ball, Ball 2 is a tennis ball, and Ball 3 is a baseball. So they have different masses, arranged in this order: $M_1 < M_2 < M_3$. Molly pitches each ball in pretty much the same way, with pretty much the same force, F_{net}, exerted over the same time interval. Do the balls leave Molly's hand with the same speed? No, because according to Newton's second law, the three balls have accelerations that are inversely proportional to their masses. The smaller the mass, the larger the speed of the ball leaving Molly's hand.

When we see an acceleration of the center of mass of an object, we conclude there is a force. When the acceleration happens for an object in circular motion, the force that causes the motion is called the **centripetal force**. For a ladybug with a mass of 0.1 gram, at the end of an $R = 12$ cm second hand, Equation 5.2 says that the acceleration would have magnitude

$$a = R(2\pi/T)^2 = 0.13 \text{ cm/s}^2$$

$$F_f = Ma = 1.3 \times 10^{-7} \text{ N}$$

So F_f is less than a millionth of a Newton, something a ladybug can comfortably manage. This tiny force is parallel to the acceleration, so as discussed in Chapter 5, it would be oriented inward

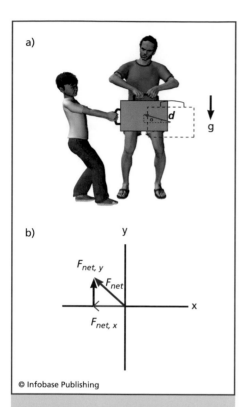

a)

b)

© Infobase Publishing

Figure 7.1 *(a) Ashok and his brother accelerate a suitcase starting at time t = 0, so that it is displaced by the vector dt at time t. Shown is t = 1/3 second. (b) The net horizontal force is due entirely to Ashok's brother pulling left. The net vertical force is the vector sum of Ashok pulling up and gravity pulling down.*

always pointing toward the center of the clock as the hand sweeps around.

TUG-OF-WAR

In Figure 7.1a, Ashok and his little brother are fighting over the suitcase that they managed to close in Chapter 6. Suppose we know the forces that Ashok and his brother exert, and the mass of the suitcase. How will it move? (This situation brings together learning from several chapters of this book.) Say that Ashok is pulling straight up with 50 N. His brother is pulling to the left with 20 N. The suitcase has a mass of 3.6 kg. To solve the problem of its motion, we will first want to draw a force-body diagram and use it to find the net force—its direction and size—on the suitcase. Equation 7.2 will then tell us the size of the acceleration. Finally, we will use the kinematic equations from Chapter 3. The net force (Figure 7.1b) has components

$$F_{net,x} = -20 \text{ N (to the left)}$$

$$F_{net,y} = 50 \text{ N} - (3.6 \text{ kg}) (9.8 \text{ m/s}^2) = 15 \text{ N (upward)}$$

We add the x and y components as in Chapter 4:

$$F_{net} = \sqrt{F_{net,x}{}^2 + F_{net,y}{}^2} = 25 \text{ N}$$

We can now apply Equation 7.2 to find

$$a = 25 \text{ N}/3.6\text{kg} = 6.9 \text{ m/s}^2$$

We need to know how the suitcase was moving at time $t = 0$, when the boy started pulling. Suppose it starts with a zero initial position and velocity. Then Equations 3.3 and 3.4 tell us that

$$v(t) = at$$

$$d(t) = 1/2 \ at^2$$

Both position and velocity are parallel to the acceleration, which is, as shown in Figure 7.1b, oriented at $\theta = 37°$. For example, at a time of $t = 1/3$ second:

$$v = (6.9)(1/3) \text{ m/s} = 2.3 \text{ m/s}$$

is the speed at which the case is moving.

$$d = (1/2)(6.9)(1/9) \text{ m} = 0.38 \text{ m}$$

is how far the suitcase has moved.

Ashok has lifted the suitcase up a distance of about a foot:

$$d_{up} = 0.38 \sin 37° = 0.38 \ (15/25) \text{ m} = 0.23 \text{ m}$$

and his little brother has pulled sideways a bit farther than that:

$$d_{sideways} = 0.38 \cos37° = 0.38 \ (20/25) \ m = 0.31 \ m$$

UNDERSTANDING THAT VELOCITY IS RELATIVE

It will prove helpful to Molly, when she describes the motion of Bai Lee and the bus, to choose a convenient **reference frame**. A reference frame is a location from which you judge the motion of objects around you. To determine if one of those objects is moving, how fast, and in what direction, is subjective. If that object defined your reference frame, you would consider it to be standing still!

You can prove this to yourself next time you ride in a car on a straight, smooth road. With your eyes closed and your ears plugged so you have trouble hearing road-related sounds, ask the driver to speed up and slow down a few times (just to mix you up) and then to drive at a constant velocity. Without any sound or sight-related clues, try to guess how fast you are going. You shouldn't be able to guess. Your internal motion sensors are not giving you any information, because they only detect accelerated motion; they can't distinguish one uniform speed from another. The interior of the car becomes your reference frame. There is no device we could put in your place, whether mechanical, electrical, or biological, to tell you "How fast am I going?" You can only ask it "How fast am I going relative to some other object?" For this reason, we say that velocity is relative.

The relativity of velocity can be applied to our hero at the end of Chapter 6. The way we told the story there, the hero ended up drifting at v_{bigger}, somewhat faster than v, the original speed. The book ended up moving at $v_{smaller}$, somewhat slower than v. The ship then started to leave the book behind, and the hero meanwhile caught up with the airlock door (see Figure 6.6). But we could tell an equally valid version of the story from the point of view of an alien on the ship, who is watching out a window (Figure 7.2). At first before the book is thrown, the alien sees the hero and book at rest. After it is thrown, the hero is moving toward the front of the ship, and the book toward the rear. Though the sizes of the speeds are different in the two versions, the important things remain the same. The hero is still rescued by reaching the air-lock, and the book still drifts away from aliens who might want to grab and read it.

Let's say the alien sees the hero moving at velocity v_{hero} and the book at v_{book}. The two per-spectives, ours and the alien's, are tied together in this way:

$$v_{bigger} = v + v_{hero}$$

This is called the Galilean transformation (named after the Italian physicist and astrono-mer Galileo Galilei). It is the rule for changing your defini-tion of the velocity of some ob-ject (here, the hero) when you switch frames of reference. For example, the Galilean transformation for the drifting book is

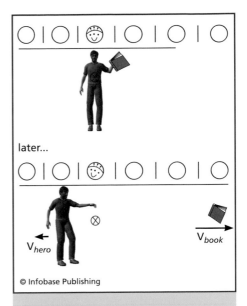

later...

© Infobase Publishing

Figure 7.2 *The situation in Figure 6.6, seen from the point of view of an alien on the ship. From this point of view, the hero travels with speed $v_{hero} = v_{bigger} - v$, whereas the book travels with speed $v_{book} = v_{smaller} - v$. The signs of these speeds are oppo-site; the hero moves left and the book moves right.*

$$v_{smaller} = v + v_{book}$$

The Galilean transformation ensures that important things like whether the hero is rescued, or whether $F = ma$, stay the same no matter what reference frame we choose. There is just one catch. Suppose you are in a frame of reference which itself is accelerating, like a bus that speeds up when a traffic light turns green. Suppose that somehow you don't know the bus is speeding up. Strange things would seem to happen. Without any force acting, a marble would begin to roll backwards down the bus aisle. The little air-freshener hanging from the windshield mirror (an accelerometer) would start to sway backwards. The surface of the water in the cup you are holding would suddenly become tilted. In unaccelerated frames, also called **inertial frames**, Newton's first law guarantees unforced motions are uniform, the Galilean transformation holds, and marbles do not start to roll on their own.

A NEW WAY TO LOOK AT MASS

At this point, we've used the concept of mass a lot, but Newton's second law gives us a new perspective. What is mass? To a chemist, your body's mass could be found from how many atoms of what kind are in your body. To a physicist from Chapter 6, mass would be found from your weight (and knowing what planet you are on). There is also another way for a physicist to think about mass. The more mass an object has, the less it will be accelerated by a force of a given size. Mass dictates how reluctant something is to be accelerated by force. A synonym for mass is **inertia**, a word that means just this.

When Molly was younger, she first began to perform her "experiments on inertia" (as her dad called them). Standing next to the dining room table, not even tall enough to see its surface, she would grab the tablecloth with both hands, pull as she stepped back, and run away laughing, leaving the tablecloth on the floor. One day, someone left the heavy phone book on the table. When Molly tried the experiment, she noticed how much more difficult it was to pull the cloth off the table and was unpleasantly surprised when along with the cloth came a huge book, narrowly missing her head as it fell onto the floor. The reason that Molly had to pull harder that day was because she was accelerating an object that consisted of two parts, the book and the cloth. This compound object had a mass equal to $(M_{book} + M_{cloth})$. Assuming that Molly tries to get roughly the same acceleration (a) as she moves back with the cloth in her hands, Molly would need to pull with a force of $M_{cloth}a$ in the absence of the book. However, with the greater force of $(M_{book} + M_{cloth})a$ in the presence of the book.

Even though astronauts in orbit experience weightlessness, they still have to undergo training to get used to manipulating extremely massive objects. An 8,000 kg metal supporting structure, drifting toward an astronaut, could easily crush him or her against the wall of the vehicle. Astronauts need to develop an instinctive respect for inertia, and the difficulty in accelerating it, before they fly a space mission.

Also part of an astronaut's training is understanding that when you push or pull an object along Earth, you are using the frictional force on your feet, from the floor, to brace yourself. But it turns out that two surfaces must exert normal forces against each other in order to produce frictional forces along each other. With no gravity pulling her down to the hull of the space station, an astronaut would not get any friction on the soles of her feet as she tries to push a solar panel into place. Her feet would just keep slipping out from under her. So astronauts have to brace themselves more methodically than they would on Earth, using special foot grips, tying themselves to objects with ropes, and so on.[23]

People naturally relate an object's heaviness to its mass, M. This is only natural, as an object's weight is equal to Mg, the gravitational force. But there is something strange about this. If you pull with a force F, since $F = Ma$, a box with a large mass will accelerate less and one with a small mass will accelerate more. How is gravity so premeditated that it "knows" to pull on a massive object more, and a light object less, in order to make their accelerations agree perfectly with the value $a = g = 9.8$ m/s^2? It is as if there is no actual gravitational force; instead, the Earth is accelerating up, past everything on it, at 9.8 m/s^2!

This brings us back to the idea of g-forces described in Chapter 5. A related concept is that of apparent weight. Suppose that a mass M is placed on a spring scale. Such scales have an internal spring that is connected to a dial. If the spring is compressed by having to support the mass, it counters by exerting the force,

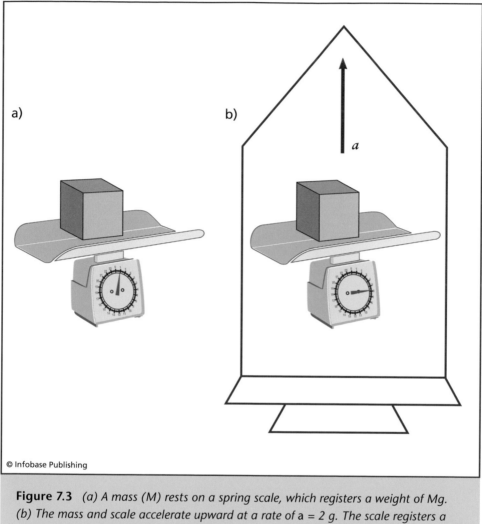

a)

b)

a

Figure 7.3 *(a) A mass (M) rests on a spring scale, which registers a weight of Mg. (b) The mass and scale accelerate upward at a rate of a = 2 g. The scale registers a new apparent weight of 3 Mg as a result.*

F_S (Table 6.1). In Figure 7.3, a mass M is placed on a spring scale, and the scale is placed in a rocket accelerating upward with $a = 2\,g$. The scale reads a weight of 1 Mg on Earth, but 3 Mg in the rocket. These values match up with the g-forces Dr. Kelp defined in Chapter 5; the g-force is g in part a of Figure 7.3 and $g + 2\,g =$

3 g in part b. Thanks to Newton's second law, we can now understand this; the spring force, F_S, will obey

$$F_S - Mg = 0, \text{ so } F_S = Mg \qquad \text{(Part } a)$$

$$F_S - Mg = Ma, \text{ so } F_S = Mg + Ma = 3 \, Mg \qquad \text{(Part } b)$$

Apparently, the spring scale, by telling you the force it exerts, is telling you the apparent weight of the box.

"Has the weight of the box really increased in part b?" is a good philosophical question. The box has the same mass (M) in both cases, so perhaps you would say no. If M were put on a planet where the gravitational field is three times that of Earth's, the scale weight would triple. Perhaps you'd argue that was a different situation than accelerating the scale. If Albert Einstein were asked, however, he would probably answer that the situations were not really different. His principle of equivalence states that since a person in the reference frame defined by the rocket can't tell the difference between being on such a planet, and the reference frame accelerating, there is no difference. Einstein would probably say that yes, in part b the box is really heavier; it has more weight.

FORCE IS A TWO-WAY STREET: NEWTON'S THIRD LAW

We were able to understand the hero of Chapter 6's clever book-throwing tactic with Newton's first law, which explains why the center-of-mass of the hero-book system stayed at rest. The situation can also be understood in terms of Newton's third law, that forces between two bodies are always equal in size and opposite in direction. Newton's third is not a law about net force, like Newton's second law. Rather, it is rather a law about individual physical forces such as the ones described in Tables 6.1 and 6.2. Suppose one object exerts a gravitational or electromagnetic force on another. We know from Newton's third law that the second body must simultaneously be exerting a force of the same size, but opposite in direction, on the first.

Let's see how this works for the hero and his book. We can take the perspective of the alien, which is simplest, since these objects start out at rest and end up with oppositely pointing velocities v_{hero} and v_{book}. Because the center-of-mass sits proportionately closer to the more massive object, the less massive object (book) would need to develop a higher speed—in fact, a speed that is directly proportionally to the ratio of the masses. In equations:

$$v_{book}/v_{hero} = m_{hero}/m_{book} \qquad (7.3)$$

You can see this in Figure 6.6; the hero is about six times more massive, so the book goes about six times farther in the same amount of time; its speed is about six times higher.

We do a little bit of algebra on Equation 7.3 to get

$$m_{book}v_{book} = m_{hero}v_{hero}$$

Taking into account that the velocity vectors v_{book} and v_{hero} are oppositely directed, let's rewrite this equation using, rather than the scalar speeds of the book and hero, their vector velocities:

$$m_{book}v_{book} = -m_{hero}v_{hero} \qquad (7.4)$$

Since the velocity is the acceleration multiplied by the time interval, Equation 7.4 means that

$$m_{book}a_{book} = -m_{hero}a_{hero} \qquad (7.5)$$

or in other words, using Newton's second law:

$$F_{hero\ on\ book} = -F_{book\ on\ hero} \qquad (7.6)$$

This is a statement of Newton's third law.

While we looked at this situation through the eyes of an alien, we could have done so from the perspective of any other observer looking from an inertial frame. Though we looked at a very specific pair of objects, the idea of Newton's third law is completely general. For any pair of objects, 1 and 2:

$$F_{1\ on\ 2} = -F_{2\ on\ 1} \tag{7.7}$$

According to Equation 7.7, when I walk, I push backward on the Earth and it pushes forward on me, and we push with completely equal and opposite forces: $F_{me\ on\ Earth} = -F_{Earth\ on\ me}$. Newton's second law would say that the reason I move forward is because the Earth pushes on me, and not the other way around. In addition, Newton's third law says that it is inevitable that if I try to push on the Earth, it will push on me, enabling my motion.

CONCLUSION: LOOK BOTH WAYS

Molly imagined a situation where a large mass, M, was moving with velocity V, bearing down on a small mass, m, darting across its path. Sitting in the park without paper or pencil, she wished that only one of the masses was moving. It would be so much easier to visualize what happened. Molly smiled as she realized that she could imagine herself, the observer, in any inertial frame she wanted. Suppose she imagined that she was riding along at velocity V, keeping pace with the big mass before the collision. In her frame of reference, using the Galilean transformation, the big mass would be at rest before the collision. The important things are the same in all inertial frames of reference. If the collision is dangerous in one frame, it is dangerous in all.

So what would happen when small mass, m, traveling at velocity, v, collided with a large stationary mass? Molly ticked off the consequences. They would exert forces on each other. According to Newton's third law, the forces would be equal and opposite. According to Newton's second law, each object would accelerate under the influence of the force. Moreover, though the forces were the same size, it was clear to Molly that the accelerations would not be the same.

Thinking about the magnitudes of force and acceleration, the following went through Molly's head:

$$\text{Collision force} = F_{big\ on\ small} = F_{small\ on\ big} = ma_{small\ mass} = Ma_{big\ mass}$$

If M was huge, the big mass would hardly accelerate. A bus that began at speed V would pretty much keep that speed after the collision. In Molly's chose frame of reference, it would start at rest and stay at rest. The small mass, however, might accelerate enormously because

$$a_{small\ mass} = \text{collision force}/m$$

For a fixed collision force, the smaller the value of m, the greater the value of its acceleration.

How big was the collision force? Did it depend on M, m, and v? Here, Molly had to use her common sense. In the limit where M was very much bigger than m, the small object might bounce off the big one like a highly elastic ball off a hard floor. It would come out with pretty much the speed that it came in, maybe a little less, but probably not so much less that she would get a wildly inaccurate estimate of the force this way. Reasoning this way, the change in speed of the little mass would be $2v$.

If Molly could calculate how long it took for the collision to occur, δt, she could calculate the acceleration during that collision as:

$$a = \delta v/\delta t = 2v/\delta t$$

Then she could say that the force (really the average force during the time of the collision) was

$$\text{Collision force} = ma = 2\ mv/\delta t \qquad (7.8)$$

How long, δt, did the collision take? It probably took about as long as it took for the little mass to cover a distance equal to its width. At this point, Molly was ready to put in numbers for sizes and speeds. For the speeds, she used the ones that she and Bai Lee had mentioned. The little mass was darting across the street with a speed of 5 miles/hour and the big mass was moving along the street at 20 miles/hour. Molly realized that she had to do the calculation in the frame of reference where the big mass was stationary. To find the velocity, **v**, of Bai Lee relative to the bus, she needed to add the bus's velocity to Bai Lee's velocity, both measured relative to

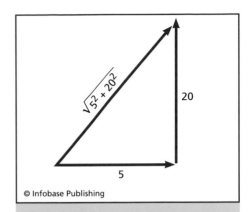

Figure 7.4 *Molly scratches a similar diagram in the sand in order to visualize the sum of two velocities.*

the street. This is just the Galilean transformation. Molly took a stick and scratched the following picture (Figure 7.4) in the sandy dirt in order to do this. She saw that it was easy to add the velocity vectors in this case, because they were at right angles. The picture let her see that she just needed the hypotenuse of the right triangle she had drawn:

$$v = \sqrt{5^2 + 20^2} \text{ miles/hr} \approx 21 \text{ miles/hr}$$

Molly wanted to convert between miles and hours and meters and seconds so she could get the force in Newtons. Fortunately, since the dirt was not a very good medium for doing a lot of arithmetic, it was a conversion whose approximate value she remembered:

$$1 \text{ mile/hour} = 1/2 \text{ meter/sec}$$

In other words, $v \approx 11$ meters/sec. The collision would last as long as it took an object traveling at 11 meters/sec to cross a distance that was the size of the little mass. Suppose this object was roughly 1 foot wide. This would be around $\delta d = 0.3$ meters. So the time would be the distance divided by the speed:

$$\delta t = \delta d / v = 0.3 \text{ m} / 11 \text{ m/s} = 0.03 \text{ s}$$

Molly felt like she was using every scrap of physics she knew (indeed, she was borrowing from every chapter in this book). But she was nearing the end. She could see that the short time, $\delta t = 0.03$ seconds, would lead to a very large force. She knew it not only from the physics in Equation 7.8 but also from highway safety class, where they learned that the purpose of bumpers on vehicles was to extend the time of a collision so the collision force between two vehicles ended up smaller.

From Equation 7.8, since collision force was $2 \, mv/\delta t$, if Molly plugged in a mass like $m = 24$ kg for the small mass she got

Collision force = 2 × 24 kg × 11 m/s/0.03 s = 17,600 N

Thinking of this in human terms, namely, the acceleration due to gravity or g-forces, this was very large:

Collisional g-force = 17,600 N/24 kg/9.8 m/s^2 ≈ 75 g

From her Highway Safety class, Molly knew that people could safely withstand only up to around this amount, approximately 80g, though it also depended on how long the force acted.

Molly was surprised when she looked up from the gloomy calculation and saw Bai Lee standing expectantly before her, tired of the playground and eager to go home. She readied herself to give Bai Lee a short lecture on, if not the physics of force and motion, at least pedestrian safety. But before she could begin, Bai Lee took her hand and said calmly, "Let me help you, Molly—I will teach you how to look both ways and cross when there is no traffic."

Notes

1. Stephen Frautschi, Richard P. Olenick, Tom M. Apostol and David L. Goodstein, *The Mechanical Universe*. Cambridge: Cambridge University Press, 1986, p. 3.
2. James Gleick, *Isaac Newton*. New York: Pantheon Books, 2003.
3. Roger A. Freeman and William J. Kaufmann, III, *Universe*, 7th ed. New York: W.H. Freeman and Co., 2005, Ch. 16.
4. Freeman and Kaufmann, *Universe*, Ch. 26.
5. For an example of what such a corridor might look like, see MIT's Infinite Corridor at http://web.mit.edu/planning/www/mithenge.html.
6. The Traveling Salesman Problem. Available online at http://www.tsp.gatech.edu.
7. Parmenides, "On Nature." In Arthur Fairbanks, *The First Philosophers of Greece*. London: K. Paul, Trench, Trubner, 1898, pp. 86–135.
8. Joseph and Barbara Anderson, "The Myth of Persistence of Vision Revisited," *Journal of Film and Video*. 45(1993): 3–12.
9. Edwin A. Abbott. *Flatland: A Romance of Many Dimensions*. Available online at http://www.geom.uiuc.edu/~banchoff/Flatland.
10. Athens 2004 Olympic Games International Torch Relay. Available online at http://www.torchrelay.net/ancientolympia/index.html.
11. Wolfram Mathworld. "Uniform Circular Motion." Available online at http://mathworld.wolfram.com/UniformCircularMotion.html.
12. Robert Ehrlich, *The Cosmological Milkshake: A Semi-Serious Look at the Size of Things*. New Brunswick: Rutgers University Press, 1995, Ch. 14.
13. Merriam-Webster Online. Available at http://www.m-w.com.
14. Gerard t'Hooft, *In Search of the Ultimate Building Blocks*. Cambridge: Cambridge University Press, 1997.
15. Harold Levin, *Contemporary Physical Geology*, 3rd ed. Philadelphia: Saunders College Publishing, 1990.
16. David Park, *The How and the Why*. Princeton: Princeton University Press, 1988, pp. 47–50, p. 211.
17. Jean-Louis and Monique Tassoul, *A Concise History of Solar and Stellar Physics*. Princeton: Princeton University Press, 2004.
18. Dan Russell. "Acoustics Animations: Motion of the Center of Mass." Available online at http://www.kettering.edu/~drussell/Demos/COM/com-a.html.
19. Susan Scott, "Ocean Watch: Mysterious Sea Creatures Delight with Dazzling Lights." Available online at http://www.susanscott.net/OceanWatch2001/oct26–01.html.
20. Adrian Bejan and James Marden, "Constructing Animal Locomotion from New Thermodynamics Theory," *American Scientist*. 94(2006): 342–349.
21. Geoffrey A. Landis. "Human Exposure to Vacuum." Available online at

http://www.sff.net/people/
Geoffrey.Landis/vacuum
.html.

22. NASA's Imagine the Universe! Ask an Astrophysicist. Available online at
http://imagine.gsfc.nasa.
gov/docs/ask_astro/
answers/970603.html.

23. NASA Human Space
Flight. Space Station
Extravehicular Activity.
Available online at http://
spaceflight.nasa.gov/
station/eva/index.html.

GLOSSARY

ACCELERATED MOTION   Motion during which the instantaneous velocity is changing.

ACCELERATION   The vector which gives the direction of, and the instantaneous rate at which velocity changes with time.

AVERAGE ACCELERATION   The change in velocity during a time interval, divided by that time interval.

AVERAGE VELOCITY   The displacement in a time interval, divided by that time interval.

ACTION-AT-A-DISTANCE FORCE   A fundamental force of nature that is seemingly transmitted over empty space.

AVERAGE SPEED   The straight-line distance between the endpoints of a motion, divided by its duration in time.

CENTER-OF-MASS   The average location for all the mass in a given object, or set of objects.

CENTRIPETAL FORCE   A force toward the center of a circular motion, which is needed to keep an object in circular motion.

CONTACT FORCE   A nonfundamental force of nature that can be traced to the physical touching of two objects.

DIMENSIONS   The type of physical property that a number or variable represents. Examples include length, mass, and time.

DISPLACEMENT   The vector that joins two subsequent positions of an object.

DYNAMICS   The study of motion as produced by forces.

FORCE   An influence that, if applied to a free body, results in an acceleration of the body.

FORCE-BODY DIAGRAM   A technique of making a simplified drawing of the individual force vectors acting on an object.

FREE FALL   A condition in which an object is accelerated only by the attraction of gravity.

GRAVITATIONAL FIELD   A quantity, usually symbolized as g, with a value equal to the gravitational acceleration, usually of a planet.

INERTIA   A synonym for mass; this is the resistance of an object to being accelerated by a force.

INERTIAL FRAME   A frame of reference in which Newton's first law holds.

INSTANTANEOUS SPEED   The size of the velocity vector.

KINEMATICS   The study of motion, without consideration of what causes it.

MASS   The physical bulk in an object.

MECHANICS   The branch of physics that deals with the effects of matter, force, and energy as they are applied to objects.

NET FORCE   A vector quantity that is the sum of all the separate, distinct forces on an object.

PATH LENGTH   The length of the actual, physical path traversed by an object (as opposed to the straight-line distance between the endpoints).

POINT MASS   A hypothetical object in which all the physical bulk is concentrated in a tiny, point-sized location.

PRESSURE   The force on an object per unit area of a surface.

PROJECTILE   An object that follows a path determined by gravity (and perhaps air resistance) near the surface of the Earth.

RANGE   The horizontal distance that a projectile travels during its flight.

REFERENCE FRAME   A location or, more abstractly, a set of axes against which position or motion can be measured and interpreted.

SCALAR   A nonvector quantity; a number or algebraic symbol that has a size, but no direction.

SYSTÈME INTERNATIONALE (SI)   A system of units developed in 1960 with worldwide use.

TRAJECTORY   The path of an object moving through space.

UNIFORM CIRCULAR MOTION   A motion in which an object travels in a circle with a fixed center and radius, at a fixed speed.

UNIFORM MOTION   A motion that proceeds at the same speed and in the same direction.

UNITS   One of many possible specific, systematized choices for writing the dimensions of a quantity. For example, the dimension of mass can be written in units of grams or kilograms.

VECTOR   A quantity that has both a size and a direction.

VELOCITY   The vector which gives the direction of and the instantaneous rate at which the displacement of an object changes with time.

WEIGHT   The force with which the planet's gravity is pulling down on an object.

BIBLIOGRAPHY

Ford, Kenneth. *Basic Physics.* Lexington, Mass.: Xerox College Publishing, 1968.

Kleppner, Daniel, and Robert Kolenkow. *An Introduction to Mechanics.* Boston: McGraw Hill, 1973.

Wolfson, Richard. *Essential University Physics.* New York: Benjamin Cummings, 2007.

FURTHER READING

Cassidy, David, Gerard Holton, and James Rutherford. *Understanding Physics*. New York: Springer-Verlag, 2002.

Ehrlich, Robert. *The Cosmological Milkshake*. New Brunswick: Rutgers University Press, 1995.

Eisenkraft, Arthur. *Active Physics*. Armonk, N.Y.: It's About Time Publishers, 2005.

Schwartz, Cindy. *A Tour of the Subatomic Zoo*. New York: AIP Press, 1996.

Wertheim, Margaret. *Pythagoras' Trousers*. Toronto: Random House, 1995.

Web Sites

ActivPhysics Online
http://wps.aw.com/aw_young_physics_11/0,8076,898586-,00.html

How Stuff Works
http://www.howstuffworks.com/

M.I.T. Open Courseware in Physics
http://ocw.mit.edu/OcwWeb/Physics/

Physics Applets, University of Oregon Department of Physics
http://jersey.uoregon.edu/vlab/

Physics Tutoring: Mechanics, Salt Lake Community College
http://ww2.slcc.edu/schools/hum_sci/physics/tutor/2210/index.html

Physlets
http://webphysics.davidson.edu/Applets/Applets.html

The Physics Classroom
Web Physics, Indiana University Purdue University at Indianapolis
http://webphysics.iupui.edu/

PICTURE CREDITS

Index

ABOUT THE AUTHOR

AMY BUG is Professor of Physics and past Department Chair in the Department of Physics and Astronomy at Swarthmore College. She graduated from Williams College in 1979 with a B.A. in physics and mathematics, and received her Ph.D. in physics in 1984 from the Massachusetts Institute of Technology. She has done collaborative research at Exxon Research and Engineering Company, Columbia University, the University of Pennsylvania, and Lawrence Livermore National Laboratory. Her research is in the area of computational chemical physics. She also studies issues of gender, race and science. She has two wonderful sons, Murphy and Moses. She would like to dedicate this book to her mother and father, and to Dr. Kelp.

ABOUT THE EDITOR

DAVID G. HAASE is Professor of Physics and Director of The Science House at North Carolina State University. He earned a B.A. in physics and mathematics at Rice University and an M.A. and Ph.D. in physics at Duke University, where he was a J. B. Duke Fellow, and has been an active researcher in experimental low temperature and nuclear physics. Dr. Haase is the founding Director of The Science House (www.science-house.org), which annually serves more than 3,000 teachers and 20,000 students across North Carolina. He has co-authored over 120 papers in experimental physics and in science education, and has co-edited one book of student learning activities and five volumes of *Conference Proceedings on K-12 Outreach from University Science Departments*. Dr. Haase has received the Distinguished Service Award of the North Carolina Science Teachers Association and was chosen 1990 Professor of the Year in the State of North Carolina by the Council for the Advancement and Support of Education (CASE).